DIALECTICAL BEHAVIOR THERAPY

DBT SKILLS WORKBOOK FOR TEENS

A fun guide to manage anxiety and
stress, understand your emotions and
learn effective communication

A FREE GIFT TO OUR READERS

YOU GET:

✓ PRINTABLE WORKSHEETS: DBT Skills Workbook for Teens Worksheets

✓ BONUS EBOOK: DBT Skills for Parents of Teenagers – 10 DBT tools to better connect with and help your teenager thrive

To get exclusive access to these FREE bonuses, go to https://www.teen-thrive.com/dbt

Feel free to contact us at hello@teen-thrive.com

TABLE OF CONTENTS

FOREWORD

On a daily basis, I sit face to face with a range of young people experiencing the agony and complex pains of trying to understand themselves and forge a path from childhood into adulthood. If they have found their way into my office, it typically means that they have been having an especially rough go of this vulnerable development time. As a Dialectical Behavior (DBT) therapist who has specialized in working with suicidal, self-injurious, and emotionally dysregulated youth for the past decade, I have watched with the rest of the western world as the demand for my services has increased. The data have confirmed that the rates of adolescent hospitalizations, self-injury, anxiety and depression have indeed risen over the past decade. As a teen, parent or other professional, you are likely personally aware of the emotional, interpersonal and social challenges of adolescence. Today's youth need a broader and more complex set of strategies to help them with their emotional struggles and work toward greater well being.

The creator of DBT, Marsha Linehan, was always very clear that DBT is "not a suicide prevention program" but a "life improvement program." The skills and strategies taught in DBT are not just about preventing destructive behaviors when in emotional crises, but building strong emotional hygiene. At its core, DBT skills are about how to build a meaningful life, allowing emotions to be a constructive part of that picture without derailing the project. The skills of DBT can help a range of youth, from those struggling with "typical" challenges of growing up to those experiencing extreme emotional distress.

I often hesitate to "assign" books/workbooks to teens because I know most experience it as being an extension of school work. Furthermore, most workbooks for youth are "adapted" from adult materials, but not formed from the start with the mindset of what teens find appealing. When I first opened this book, I was taken aback by how it was unlike any other workbook I had seen before. The graphics are eye-catching, the activities are engaging. This workbook guides you through a compelling story about what DBT is, where it came from, and how to apply it to your life. For adolescents that have had exposure to DBT before, this workbook breathes fresh life into familiar concepts.

The contents of this book break down crucial skills and teaching into fun and digestible chunks that youth can work through with their families, their therapists, or on their own. This workbook is unique in a sea of teen "self-help" materials because you, the teen, are not a mere passive recipient of the book's information, but an active participant in the process of learning. We professionals know that learning by "doing" provides the most robust and enduring outcomes. The opportunities to practice these skills in a variety of ways is integrated throughout the book's structure. It addresses all the key areas in DBT skills training: increasing awareness of yourself and your environment, acting wise in the face of distress, improving emotional resilience, and navigating relationships.

Those of us concerned about youth and families in distress know that getting them the support that they need is often easier said than done. Some families struggle to get access to the specialists needed. Some have had so many poor experiences that they are skeptical of therapy all together. Many teens have fatigue around therapy; bored of the repetitive conversations around emotions and the tired lists of "coping skills." You may be an adolescent who would rather get tips from social media than from books written by well-known professionals because the content is vastly more relatable. This book is a welcome resource to help build confidence in building the life you want and taking on life challenges, both the typical and extraordinary.

Kristen Dahlin, Ph.D.
Psychologist
DBT Center of San Diego

Being a teenager is hard. There's no doubt about it. It's the most challenging phase of life. It's when you leave behind the comfort of childhood and make your way towards adulthood.

It's a strange experience. Your body is in metamorphosis; changing, growing, rearranging. It's you against the world, a world that just doesn't seem to understand you.

The challenge is real.

But it doesn't have to be so hard. There are ways and means to make life easier for yourself. And I would be happy to share them with you.

But first, you need to complete four quests. At the end of each quest, you'll be rewarded with a bonus skill that you can use for the rest of your life.

INTRODUCTION

This isn't just a book; it's a workbook. It uses dialectical behavior therapy (DBT), a form of therapy that helps people find the balance between accepting themselves and changing what they don't like about themselves.

What's with the quests?

The four quests in the book are designed to empower you with skills you can use in the real world:

Discover your inner focus to harness the powers of your mind and channel them appropriately.

Train in distress endurance to be prepared for anything that comes your way.

Surf the sea of emotions to truly understand your emotions and reign over them.

Master the art of conversation at Communication Caves to connect with those around you and communicate effectively.

But I don't need therapy!

Yes, Dr. Marsha Linehan indeed developed DBT to help those with mental health issues. But, over time, it has come to benefit anyone and everyone. The techniques taught in DBT can make your journey into adulthood smoother. And it can also make the rest of your life much easier.

Who can use this book?

This book is for both teenagers and their families. Parents and guardians can also use this workbook to learn strategies to effectively communicate with teenagers and improve their relationships.

While this book offers accurate worksheets and exercises recommended by DBT, it cannot be used as an alternative to in-person therapy. If your teenager is already in therapy, it is recommended that you consult the therapist before using this workbook.

DR. MARSHA AND HER DISCOVERY

MAY 5, 1943.
TULSA, OKLAHOMA

MARSHA LINEHAN WAS BORN.

SHE WAS ONE OF SIX CHILDREN. GOOD AT SCHOOL, GREAT AT PIANO.

SHE FELT DIFFERENT FROM HER SIBLINGS,
LIKE SOMETHING WAS MISSING,
AND SHE DIDN'T BELONG.

SENIOR YEAR OF HIGH SCHOOL, SHE WAS BEDRIDDEN.
ON THE SURFACE, THERE WERE CHRONIC HEADACHES,

DISTRESS WAS RISING ON THE INSIDE.

MARCH 9, 1961,
HARTFORD, CONNECTICUT

MARSHA LINEHAN WAS ADMITTED TO A HOSPITAL.

UNHAPPY AND BROKEN.
SPIRALING DOWN HER OWN VERSION OF HELL.

SHE STAYED ALONE AND HELPLESS.

"THEY PUT ME IN
A FOUR-WALLED ROOM

BUT LEFT ME REALLY OUT

MY SOUL WAS TOSSED
SOMEWHERE ASKEW

MY LIMBS WERE TOSSED
HERE ABOUT"

MAY 31, 1963,
SHE LEFT THE HOSPITAL,

STILL CLUELESS OF
WHAT WAS AILING HER
BUT DETERMINED TO
PERSEVERE...

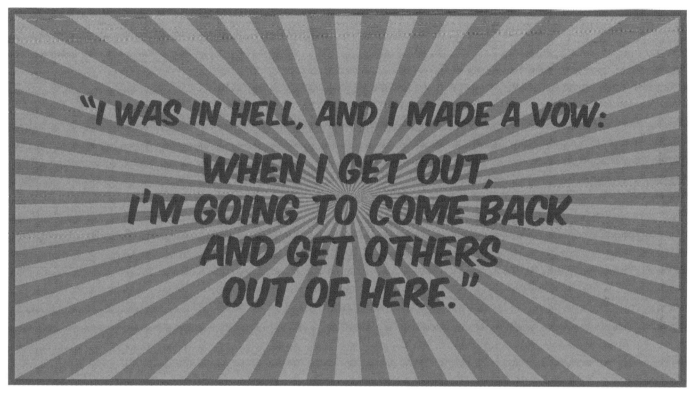

"I WAS IN HELL, AND I MADE A VOW:
WHEN I GET OUT,
I'M GOING TO COME BACK
AND GET OTHERS
OUT OF HERE."

WHILE HELLFIRE RAGED ON IN HER MIND,
SHE SEARCHED FOR ANSWERS,

BY STUDYING THE MIND.

1971, SHE RECEIVED HER DOCTORATE,

DR. MARSHA WAS BORN.

SHE BEGAN HER WORK AT A CLINIC,
TREATING THE MOST TROUBLED SOULS,
THOSE THAT THE WORLD HAD GIVEN UP ON,

THOSE WHO HAD GIVEN UP ON THEMSELVES.

IN 1967, SHE MADE A REMARKABLE DISCOVERY

FOUR POWERS THAT COMBINE TO FORM THE BALANCE BETWEEN ACCEPTANCE AND CHANGE

MINDFULNESS TO FOCUS

ENDURANCE TO SURVIVE

CONTROL OVER EMOTIONS

POWERFUL COMMUNICATION

ORIENTATION

Welcome to orientation.

This shouldn't take too long; just a few things to keep in mind as you go about your quests.

The quests must be completed in order.

A badge in each quest is mandatory for entry into the next destination.

◎ At each destination, a guide will be waiting to take you through the activities.

   ▲ Discover your inner focus with Guru Dave at Mindfulness Mountain

   ▇ Train in distress endurance with Sergeant Dawson at Distress Desert

   ★ Surf the sea of emotions with Retired Captain DB Turner at Emotion Island

   ◗ Master the art of conversation with Captcha at Communication Caves

◎ You'll be given a map and a briefing at the start of each quest. Take your time to complete the tasks and quests. This isn't a race.

◎ The rewards at the end of each quest are invaluable and will last you a lifetime.

Here's an emotion directory that you will require.

THE EMOTION DIRECTORY | A guide to help you find the exact emotion

Happy

Thrilled
Amused
Content
Calm
Loved
Affectionate
Grateful

I feel good

Confident
Focused
Passionate
Creative
Encouraged
Empowered
Brave

Excited

Inspired
Impacted
Moved
Amazed
Surprised
Interested
Enthusiastic

Afraid

Nervous
Anxious
Worried
Terrified
Shocked
Petrified

Angry

Irritated
Frustrated
Furious
Livid
Aggressive
Violent
Uncontrollable

Dull

Lost
Numb
Bored
Aimless
Tired
Exhausted

Sad

Hurt
Lonely
Disappointed
Upset
Feeling sorry
Heartbroken
Depressed
Devastated

I don't feel good

Not feeling
like myself
Broken
Insecure
Insignificant
Fragile
Guilty
Embarrassed
Humiliated
Overwhelmed

I don't like

Indifferent
Uncomfortable
Offended
Grossed out
Disturbed
Repulsed

I don't trust

Cautious
Suspicious
Skeptical
Defensive
Jealous

How to keep track of your progress

When you receive the map, observe these shapes with white spaces.

When you complete an objective, you need to fill in the white space.

At the end of the quest, you should have all the shapes filled in.

Now, you're all caught up. Go on over to your first stop, the foothills of Mindfulness Mountain, where Guru Dave is expecting you.

Good luck and see you on the other side.

QUEST 1

DISCOVER YOUR INNER FOCUS

Mindfulness, sometimes referred to as meditation, has been practiced for thousands of years across the world. When you think of meditation, you probably think of something like this. More specifically, a person sitting cross-legged with their eyes closed and hands stretched out. Most likely lost in a trance of nothingness.

But mindfulness is so much more than that. It's about achieving a higher sense of awareness. For example, what are you doing right now? You're reading this book. If you're reading the paperback, you may be holding it in your hand or have it rested on your lap. If you're reading the eBook, you're looking at a backlit screen. You're experiencing some kind of physical sensation from just reading the book!

Then, there's the temperature of the room, the position you're sitting in, the texture of the furniture, the texture of your clothes, and feeling your chest move with each breath.

There are the sounds that you can hear—a vehicle outside? A child playing? Somebody on the phone? A television? Or the hum of a fan?

You may smell a meal cooking in the kitchen or the fragrance of falling rain. You may be tasting the last meal you had or the juices of bubblegum you're chewing. You may even be shaking your leg or fidgeting with a pencil without even being aware of it.

Apart from these sensations, you're also feeling emotions—sadness, happiness, boredom? Then, there are the thoughts you're having, several of them coming and going, one after another.

All of this is happening in **one single moment.**

And now, that moment has already passed. The moment that began when you started reading this book is now long gone. The cells in your body have changed, the air around you has changed, and everything that we described in the earlier paragraphs may have also changed. The present is a whole new moment with its own sensory experiences, thoughts, and emotions.

In essence, mindfulness is about being aware of your thoughts, emotions, physical sensations, and more at any given moment. It isn't humanly possible to be mindful of every little thing all the time, so don't get overwhelmed with the idea of having to do so.

▲ Be conscious of your thoughts and emotions and the behaviors that they result in
▲ Observe the effects of your behavior and identify what needs to change
▲ Let go of trying to avoid, criticize or stop the experience

This may seem like a lot of hippie babble to you, but mindfulness techniques are actually clinically used to treat chronic pain and anxiety. Learning them can help you lower stress and remain calm in the toughest of situations.

What's in it for you?

People, both teenagers, and adults, tend to become very passive in their lives. They may zone out and just do things out of habit as if they're running on autopilot. When an unexpected situation comes along, they're caught off guard by it and may experience moments of anxiety and frustration.

For example

You're making yourself a bowl of cereal, like you do every morning.
You get a text from a friend, and you stop to answer it.
When you return to continue making your cereal, you forget whether you've already added the sugar.

This is a result of being **unmindful**.

Check the ones that have happened to you!
☐ You walked to school this morning, but you can't remember actually doing it.
☐ You're attending class, and your mind begins to wander. When you "come back" to class, you have no idea what the teacher is talking about.
☐ You're having an argument with a friend, and you're already cooking up the rebuttal in your head before they're done talking.
☐ You follow a train of thought in your head while reading. When you resume focus, you need to start reading from the beginning all over again.
☐ You walk into a room to get something but forget what it was.

☐ You put something away in one of your drawers and moments later, can't remember which one.

☐ You're washing dishes and thinking of something else; you end up washing the same dish for too long.

☐ You're playing a song on a musical instrument, and you lose track of where you are in the song.

☐ You open your laptop to do one task but end up doing something completely different and realize only later.

☐ You zone out while taking a shower and forget whether you've washed your hair or not.

I bet some of them sound familiar. This is why Mindfulness Mountain is our first stop.

Welcome, friend.

I'm Guru Dave, and I'll be guiding you through Mindfulness Mountain.

Many missions await you here, exercises that will help you discover your inner focus. At the summit, I'll hand you a badge of honor and a special reward.

I wish you all the best for this quest.

G.Dave

Discover your inner focus at Mindfulness Mountain

1. Observation
2. Awareness
3. Balance
4. Relaxation

Complete the objectives in order.

Upon completion of the objective, **do not forget to fill in the triangle**.

You need all four triangles filled in to complete this quest and collect your reward.

OBJECTIVE 1: OBSERVATION

Think of your mind like a web browser where each thought is a tab. At any given moment, you may have plenty of tabs open.

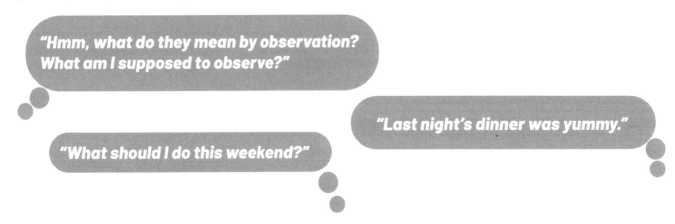

"Hmm, what do they mean by observation? What am I supposed to observe?"

"Last night's dinner was yummy."

"What should I do this weekend?"

Sometimes one thought can even lead you to other thoughts, and you go down a rabbit hole and end up with multiple tabs open.

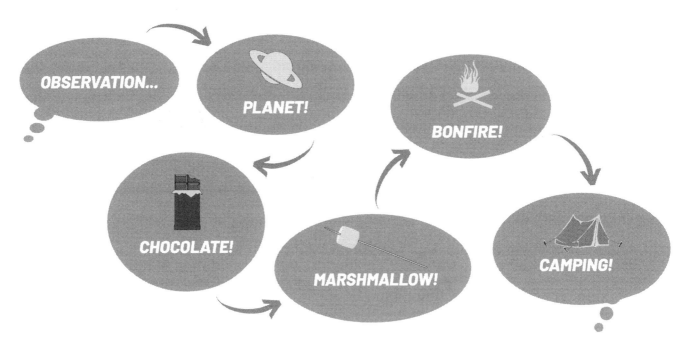

OBSERVATION...

PLANET!

BONFIRE!

CHOCOLATE!

MARSHMALLOW!

CAMPING!

But what if you had the power to keep that browser of your mind organized? Just a few tabs open; you know exactly what they are and why they're open.

What if, when your mind begins to wander to unnecessary places, you're able to bring it back to what needs attention, stay focused, and not go down the rabbit hole?

To attain this level of inner focus, you need to master the skill of observation, and that is the aim of this objective.

MISSION 1: A MINUTE'S REST

2 mins

You will need:

▲ A watch
▲ A comfortable space where you won't be disturbed

Please read the instructions before you begin.

Instructions

1. Look at the time on your watch and put it away.

2. Don't look at a clock or count the seconds. Just sit in that position for one minute

3. When you think a minute is up, look up the time.

Results

Time you put away the watch:

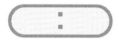

Time you picked up the watch:

Did you get it right? Was it a minute?   If not, was it <u>more</u> or <u>less</u>?   MORE ▲ ☐   LESS ▼ ☐

By how many seconds or minutes were you off?

Note the difference in time:

Conclusion

How do you perceive time? Did time go faster than you thought it would? Or did it go slower? Our perception of time impacts how we make use of it.

If we feel like we've got a lot of time, we tend to schedule more tasks and are always a little late. On the other hand, if we feel like we don't have enough time, we may go over our tasks too quickly and not do them correctly.

Keep an eye on the clock, just to see how long you take to do everyday things like taking a shower, making your bed or having breakfast.

Being mindful of time can give us the best of both worlds—we can plan our time more accurately to meet a deadline and do a good job of the task.

Tip: Come back to this exercise when you've finished all the quests to see if you can beat your high score.

MISSION 2: THINGAMAJIG

You will need:

▲ A timer (you can use a phone)
▲ A comfortable space where you won't be disturbed
▲ An object - anything tangible that you can pick up, touch, and feel with your hands.

10 mins

Pick something that you have no real attachment to; something random that you use every day.

Please read the instructions before you begin.

Instructions

1. Take a deep breath.

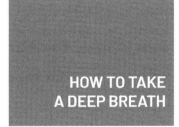

| HOW TO TAKE A DEEP BREATH | INHALE THROUGH YOUR NOSE | HOLD FOR FIVE SECONDS | EXHALE THROUGH YOUR MOUTH WHILE MAKING AN 'O' SHAPE |

2. Set the timer for five minutes and begin observing the object that you've chosen. Think of as many ways as you can to describe it. Here are some cues:

WHAT SHAPE IS IT?

WHAT COLOR IS IT?

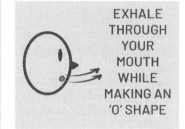
HOW BIG IS IT?

IS IT SHINY OR DULL?

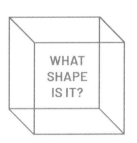

DOES IT MAKE A SOUND?

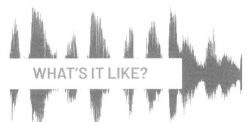
WHAT'S IT LIKE?

21

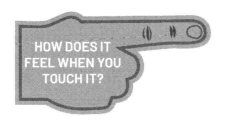

HOW DOES IT FEEL WHEN YOU TOUCH IT?

HEAVY? OR LIGHT?

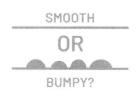

SMOOTH OR BUMPY?

DOES IT HAVE A SMELL? WHAT'S IT LIKE?

IS IT EDIBLE? WHAT DOES IT TASTE LIKE?

3. Also, notice your experience of the object. Here are some cues:

▲ How do you feel while observing this object?

▲ Does the object remind you of anything?

▲ Are there any changes in your body?

Don't get alarmed or frustrated if your mind wanders; it definitely will. Five minutes is a long time to observe a single object. Observe the thoughts that come up but try not to engage with them. Instead, try to bring your focus back to the object.

Not getting distracted isn't the aim of mindfulness. The objective is to practice regaining the focus.

4. When the timer goes off, make a note of your observations in the log. Repeat the exercise using two other objects.

Date	Object	Object description	Experience description

Conclusion

The goal of this mission was to get your mind to focus on one thing. The more time you spend doing this exercise, the easier it'll become. Just like a basketball player exercises their throws, or a chess grandmaster exercises their mind, it takes practice to become an expert in focus.

HOW IS THIS USEFUL?

Being a teenager in the digital age is no joke. There are so many distractions—games, movies, tv shows, comics, books, anime—available at the click of a button.

That's a lot of distractions dragging your focus away from things that need to get done— school work, sports, music or dance practice, or yes, even chores. The more you get distracted, the longer it takes for them to get done!

But if you could channel all of your focus on one thing, you'd finish it a lot faster and have more time to enjoy what you like doing. Observation is the first step to achieving that level of focus. Being observant of time and paying attention to the details of your tasks can help you finish them more efficiently.

Objective completed. Don't forget to fill in the triangle.

OBJECTIVE 2: AWARENESS

In your last mission, you observed an object and described it in your log. You also described any emotions, thoughts, and physical sensations that came up. That was a sneak peek into what you're going to do in this objective.

To achieve mindfulness, you need to be aware of everything that's happening. At any given point, you're experiencing the following:

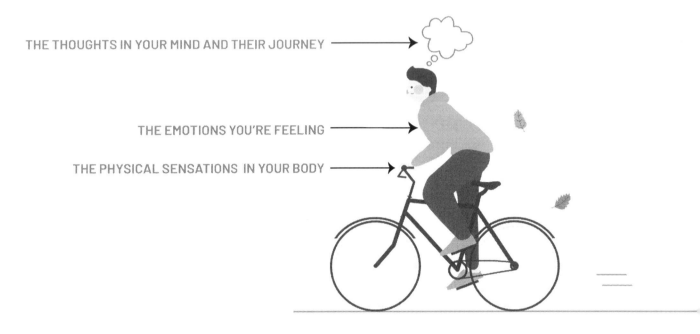

THE THOUGHTS IN YOUR MIND AND THEIR JOURNEY

THE EMOTIONS YOU'RE FEELING

THE PHYSICAL SENSATIONS IN YOUR BODY

The mission of these objectives is to focus on each of these and become aware of them. Once you're aware of them, you can decide what you need to focus on and what you can ignore.

Think of these exercises like organizing those tabs in the browser that is your mind. Those tabs are research for homework, your inbox and messengers, and some videos you want to watch. You arrange them so you can switch between them with ease. This is the same thing that we're going to do with different parts of our experience.

MISSION 1: UNDER THE SCANNER

10+ mins

You will need:

▲ A quiet, comfortable space where you won't be disturbed
▲ A bed or a mat to lie down on

Make sure the room is as quiet as it can be. Read the instructions thoroughly before you begin.

Instructions

1. Lie down face up. Make sure your arms and feet are apart and not touching each other.

2. Close your eyes. Start by taking a few deep breaths. Imagine that you're under a scanner, and it's emitting a ray of light, a small spotlight of sorts.

3. The light moves from one part of your body to another, starting at your feet and going all the way up to your head. When the light falls on a body part, channel all your focus on it and become aware of how it is feeling.

For example

The scanner first scans your feet. Imagine your toes, your sole, the top of your feet, your heels and ankles and the skin around them. How do they feel? What about your muscles and ligaments? Do you feel any pain? Do they feel tense?

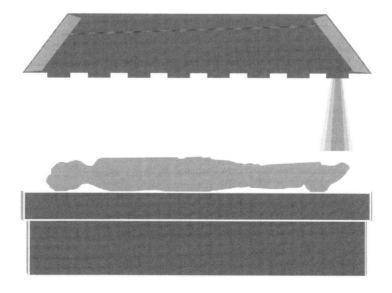

4. Once you're done being aware of how your feet feel, move on to the next part. Here is a possible route you can take:

5. When the scan is complete, take a few deep breaths and open your eyes.

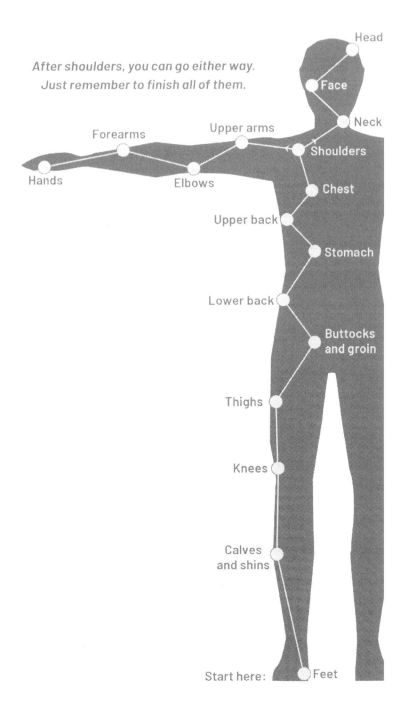

After shoulders, you can go either way. Just remember to finish all of them.

Head

Face

Neck

Upper arms

Forearms

Shoulders

Hands

Elbows

Chest

Upper back

Stomach

Lower back

Buttocks and groin

Thighs

Knees

Calves and shins

Start here: Feet

Conclusion

The goal of this exercise is to bring your attention to the physical experience. It'll help you become aware of how your body is feeling and if there's anything that needs your attention. Body scanning can also help you relax and free your body of some tension.

Complete this exercise every day for one week.						
Day 1 ☐	Day 2 ☐	Day 3 ☐	Day 4 ☐	Day 5 ☐	Day 6 ☐	Day 7 ☐

Tip: A good time to do this exercise is bedtime.

MISSION 2: THOUGHT EXPRESS

3 mins

You will need:

▲ A timer (you can use a phone)
▲ A comfortable space where you won't be disturbed
▲ A notebook and pencil OR a laptop/tablet/phone

Please read the instructions before you begin.

Instructions

1. Set the timer for three minutes.

2. Start making a note of every thought you have. You don't have to put down the entire thought, just a word or phrase.

3. Try to put down as many as you can. If you start thinking of this exercise, put down 'exercise.' Let yourself go. Remember, nobody's going to see this, and you can even delete/erase it when you're done.

4. When the timer goes off, count the number of thoughts and make a note here: _____

Conclusion

How many thoughts did you have in three minutes? Now multiply that by twenty to get an idea of how many thoughts you have in one hour.

The thought express is on its journey during every waking moment. This mission's goal was to bring your attention to just how many thoughts you can have at a given moment and how quickly they can change.

MISSION 3: THE WHEEL OF FEELING

You will need:

▲ Writing or drawing instruments
▲ Coloring instruments of your choice
▲ A print-out of the exercise sheet [if you're using an ebook] OR a sheet of paper

Please read the instructions before you begin.

 Warning: This may feel silly.

Instructions

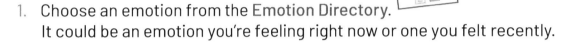

1. Choose an emotion from the Emotion Directory.
   It could be an emotion you're feeling right now or one you felt recently.

   EMOTION: _____

2. Describe the emotion with a drawing. It could be anything—scribbles, coloring, doodles, or a full-fledged drawing.

3. Fill out the questionnaire.

What is an action that you associate with this emotion? What do you generally do when you feel this emotion?

_____

_____

_____

What does this emotion sound like? Describe the sound that you associate with the emotion.

_____

_____

_____

How intensely are you feeling the emotion? You can use the scale or just describe the intensity.

1   10

_____

_____

What are the thoughts that come when you feel this emotion?

_____

_____

_____

Is there any other way you'd like to describe this emotion?

_____

_____

Conclusion

When you feel an emotion, you're not just feeling it. You're also associating it with different things, experiencing it completely—with your body and mind. And this happens with every emotion you feel. The aim of this mission was to show you how complex the experience of feeling an emotion is.

Try this exercise with two more emotions from the directory.

EMOTION 1: _____

Describe the emotion with a drawing. It could be anything—scribbles, coloring, doodles, or a full-fledged drawing.

Fill out the questionnaire.

What is an action that you associate with this emotion? What do you generally do when you feel this emotion?

_____

_____

_____

What does this emotion sound like? Describe the sound that you associate with the emotion.

_____

_____

_____

How intensely are you feeling the emotion? You can use the scale or just describe the intensity.

1   10

_____

_____

What are the thoughts that come when you feel this emotion?

_____

_____

_____

Is there any other way you'd like to describe this emotion?

_____

_____

EMOTION 2: _____

Describe the emotion with a drawing. It could be anything—scribbles, coloring, doodles, or a full-fledged drawing.

Fill out the questionnaire.

What is an action that you associate with this emotion? What do you generally do when you feel this emotion?

_____

_____

_____

What does this emotion sound like? Describe the sound that you associate with the emotion.

_____

_____

_____

How intensely are you feeling the emotion? You can use the scale or just describe the intensity.

1   10

_____

_____

What are the thoughts that come when you feel this emotion?

_____

_____

_____

HOW IS THIS USEFUL?

Remember all those distractions? The games, movies, and cartoons? Turns out there's a lot more of them.

Think of the protagonist in one of those martial arts movies. She is one person fighting so many people coming at her from all sides. She has to plan her moves in a way that she defeats everybody without hurting herself. She has to concentrate on fighting one of them but also be aware of where everybody else is.

Using your mind to focus employs a similar tactic. At any given moment, you're experiencing physical sensations, multiple emotions, and thinking about many, many things. For you to be able to focus, you need to be aware of everything. Once you have all of this information, you can decide what to focus on, for how long, what's next in line, what's unnecessary, etc.

We already do this. We're constantly choosing different things to pay attention to. If you hear someone call your name, your attention moves to them so you can listen to what they have to say. If you get bitten by an ant on your ankle, the pain or itch brings your attention to it.

But sometimes, things can steal attention.

For example

You're texting a friend, and another friend who's sitting next to you starts talking about raccoons. You may accidentally include the word 'raccoon' in your text. This happens because your focus is caught between texting your friend and listening to the other.

Awareness can help streamline the focus. You can spend all of your focus on one thing and then get to the next quickly.

Objective completed. Don't forget to fill in the triangle.

OBJECTIVE 3: BALANCE

In the last objective, we learned to focus on one thing at a time—physical sensations, thoughts, and emotions. In this objective, we add another part of experience into the mix—sensory perception.

Sensory perception is using our five senses to observe and interact with the outside world.

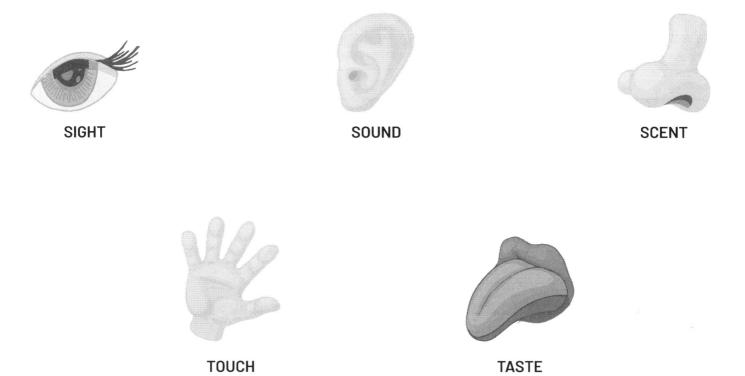

SIGHT   SOUND   SCENT

TOUCH   TASTE

This objective will train you to focus on two things simultaneously in a balanced manner. You'll focus on things within you and on the outside world while spending the same amount of time on each.

This is an essential skill because we can't really go about life separating aspects of our experiences and focusing on them one at a time. Sometimes these aspects may even go hand in hand or cause one another.

MISSION 1: INSIDE OUT

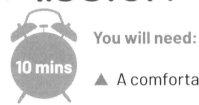

You will need:

▲ A comfortable space where you won't be disturbed

Please read the instructions before you begin.

Instructions

In this exercise, you will alternate between focusing on the outside world and the physical sensations you're experiencing. If you feel the focus shifting away from what you're observing, just calmly bring it back.

1. Take a few deep breaths before you begin.

2. Start by observing an object in the room. Observe it for a minute using only your vision. What does it look like? What shape and color is it?

3. Then turn your attention towards your own body. Remember the scanner that you used in the previous objective? Use it to find a physical sensation to focus on for a minute. It could be the weight of your body on the ground, the clenching of your jaw, a tense muscle, or an itch somewhere.

4. Next, focus on a sound and observe it for a minute. What's it like? Is it loud or soft? What's making the sound?

5. Turn your attention back to your body again and focus on another sensation for a minute.

6. Next, focus on something you can smell for a minute. Is something cooking, or is it raining? Can you smell perfume or cologne? What's the smell like? If you can't smell anything, simply observe the air going in and out of your nose.

7. Turn your attention back to your body for a minute again.

8. Next, focus on something that you can touch for a minute. It could just be a nearby object like something you're wearing or what you're sitting on. Observe its texture—is it smooth or rough? Is it hard or soft? Is it warm or cold to touch?

9. Turn your attention back to your body for the last time and observe a sensation for a minute.

10. End the exercise by taking a few deep breaths.

You can do the senses in any order you want. Just remember to alternate between a sense and your own body.

Conclusion

Our world is both around us and within us. This mission makes you focus on both while enforcing balance by not focusing on one more than the other.

MISSION 2: SENSE AND SENSITIVITY

10 mins

You will need:

▲ A comfortable space where you won't be disturbed

Please read the instructions before you begin.

Instructions

In this exercise, you'll alternate between focusing on the external world using four senses and your emotions. If you feel the focus shifting away from what you're observing, it's okay. Just calmly bring it back.

1. Take a few deep breaths before you begin.

2. Close your eyes. Start by observing how you're feeling right now and name the emotion to yourself silently. Allow the emotion to take physical form in your head and imagine what it looks like for a minute.

3. Open your eyes. Observe an object in the room for a minute using only your vision. What does it look like? What shape or color is it?

4. Close your eyes. Think of that emotion again for a minute. This time, think of a sound related to it—a noise, somebody's voice, or a song.

5. Next, observe all the sounds you can hear—things outside like a car or the wind and things inside, like a clock ticking or your dog barking.

6. When you've observed them all, return to the emotion again; this time, describe the intensity with which you feel it. Try and be as descriptive as possible. Compare it to other things (as angry as_____, sad like _____).

7. Next, observe the things that you can smell for a minute. Is something cooking? Is it raining? Can you smell perfume or cologne? What's the smell like? If you can't smell anything, simply observe the air going in and out of your nose.

8. Turn your attention back to that emotion and observe the thoughts that are coming up. Don't try to engage or reason with them; just observe them. Make sure that it's a thought and not another emotion.

9. Next, focus on something that you can touch for a minute. It could be a nearby object like something you're wearing or what you're sitting on. Observe the texture - is it smooth or rough? Is it hard or soft? Is it warm or cold to touch?

10. End the exercise by taking a few deep breaths.

For example

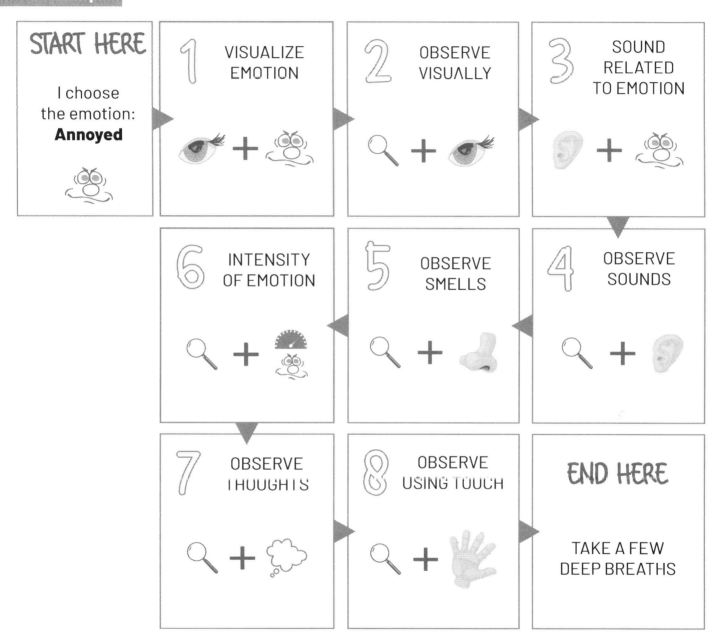

Conclusion

In this mission, we replaced physical sensations with emotions. How we're feeling at a specific moment can influence the way we perceive the outside world and vice versa.

HOW IS THIS USEFUL?

Physical sensations, thoughts, emotions, and sensory perception share a special bond. Not only can one cause another, but they can also occur together.

You <u>watch</u> a scary movie about spiders and then <u>feel</u> something crawling up your back even though there's nothing there.

You <u>eat</u> ice cream and get a <u>brain freeze</u>.

You <u>think</u> of a pet you lost and <u>feel</u> sad.

You <u>see</u> a flying cockroach, you <u>feel</u> afraid and start <u>trembling</u>.

When our focus is disproportionately on one aspect of our experience, it can cause us to respond or behave differently.

A typical example of this is an **emotional trap**.

Somebody says something mean just as you're entering school. You feel hurt by it and spend the whole day imagining comebacks. All your focus is being routed towards the incident, and you're trapped by the associated thoughts and emotions.

But with the skill of mindfulness, you can balance your focus out and simmer down quickly and easily.

Objective completed. Don't forget to fill in the triangle.

OBJECTIVE 4: RELAXATION

And we've finally arrived at the most popular destination of Mindfulness Mountain. Plenty of people come by just to learn the art of meditation because of its relaxing nature. You, my apprentice, are getting the whole package—learning the advanced version of mindfulness.

So far, you've trained to observe the different aspects of an experience; become aware of them holistically, and balance your focus between them.

However, in situations of distress, these aspects can get overwhelming. Your Thought Express is speeding, you feel physically agitated and your moods may fluctuate.

In this objective, you'll learn to declutter your experience. This can help you get a sense of clarity in moments of stress, so you can relax and respond calmly.

MISSION 1: THOUGHT EXPRESS DEACTIVATION

You will need:

3-5 mins

▲ A timer
▲ A comfortable space where you won't be disturbed

Please read the instructions before you begin.

 Warning: This may feel awkward.

Instructions

1. Set the timer for 3-5 minutes.

2. Take a few deep breaths and close your eyes.

3. Picture yourself in one of these scenarios:

You're lying on the ground and watching the clouds go by

You're driving down a highway, and billboards are going by

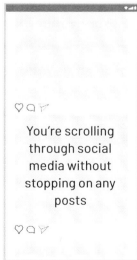

You're scrolling through social media without stopping on any posts

You're watching the end credits of a movie

In whichever scenario you choose, see your thoughts go by (on the clouds, billboards, posts, or written as credits) and keep breathing.

Don't try to stop at any of your thoughts; just let them go by. Let them appear in the form in which you think them—a picture, moving image, word, or sentence. If two thoughts appear simultaneously, let them both rise and decline together.

If a thought about the exercise crosses your mind, let that go too.

If you happen to hold on to a thought, just consciously detach yourself and let it go.

4. When the timer goes off, slowly open your eyes and return your focus to where you are.

Conclusion

This exercise, known as thought defusion, is from acceptance and commitment therapy. In situations of distress, it helps us stop going down the spiral of an unhealthy or unhappy thought. Practicing this exercise regularly can help you strain out all the unnecessary thoughts to have a clearer picture of the thoughts that matter.

MISSION 2: BREATHFLIX

"A word of advice, friend.

You may have heard of this exercise before—to concentrate on your breathing. You may have also heard people describe it as a spiritual experience.

This doesn't happen for everyone. I, too, haven't experienced it. But, I do find that it relaxes me and gives me clarity. And that is the aim of this exercise. So if you feel like you're not feeling something extraordinary, don't worry. You're not alone."

3 mins

You will need:

▲ A timer
▲ A comfortable space where you won't be disturbed

Please read the instructions before you begin.

Instructions

1. Set the timer for 3 minutes.

2. Close your eyes and lightly put one hand on your stomach.

3. Inhale through your nose, hold it for a few seconds and exhale through your mouth.

4. Focus on your breathing

Notice the way your stomach expands when you inhale and how it deflates when you exhale. Observe the air going through your nostrils and out of your mouth.

You may feel your mind wandering away—it's all right; just bring your focus back to your breathing.

Observe everything else that's happening—your lungs filling up with air, your body weighing down as you exhale.

5. Count your breaths

Start counting your breaths. You can do this aloud or just to yourself in your head. After you exhale four times, restart at one.

Slowly include focusing on your body while counting your breaths and alternate your focus between the two.

6. Thoughts and distractions

Lastly, add the observation of your thoughts and distractions.

If you find yourself going along with the Thought Express as opposed to just observing it, simply bring your focus back and count your breaths.

Remember, you're new to this, and you will get distracted. Don't be disheartened. Not getting distracted isn't the aim of mindfulness. The objective is to practice bringing the focus back.

7. When the timer goes off, open your eyes.

Conclusion

The aim of this objective was for you to tune into your breathing mindfully. Mindful breathing can help you calm down when you're feeling overwhelmed by emotion. This offers clarity to observe the situation, thoughts, and emotions and then respond to it. In essence, mindful breathing cleans up the space in your head where all of these experiences converge.

Tip: Increase the number of minutes as and when you're more comfortable.

Advanced mindful breathers can last up to 15-20 minutes. Some people can even do it while doing other activities like art, exercise, or even chores. The experts at the peak of Mindfulness Mountain do it for years at a time.

 *Do not try this at home.*

MISSION 3: THE EMOTION STATION

You will need:

▲ A comfortable space where you won't be disturbed

Please read the instructions before you begin.

Instructions

1. Close your eyes and take a few deep breaths.

2. Start by observing your breathing—feel the air going into your nostrils and out through your mouth. Notice your belly rising and falling and your body slowly calming down.

3. After four or five breaths, tune into your emotion.

   How are you feeling? Name the emotion and start to observe and describe it. If you can't put your finger on an emotion at this moment, think of a time in the recent past when you felt strongly about something and use that emotion.

   How does it feel? Does it feel good or bad? What's the best way to describe this feeling?

4. Dig deeper into how you're feeling.

   ▲ Is it one emotion, or are there other tiny little emotions?
   ▲ Is the intensity of the emotion changing the more you observe it?
   ▲ What's it like when it's intense, and what's it like when it's mellow?

   Thoughts, sensations, and your surroundings may try to distract you. It's okay; just calmly bring your focus back to the emotion.

5. Think about the situation that led to the emotion. What happened? Who said or did what? What did you do or say? Replay it in your head. Stay with the emotion. If it changes, observe the new emotion.

6. When the emotion begins to fade or go away, open your eyes and bring your focus back to where you are.

Conclusion

Tuning into your emotions can help untangle them. It can offer clarity on what you're feeling and why you're feeling it. The more you practice this exercise, the faster it becomes to tune into your emotions.

HOW IS THIS USEFUL?

The experience of the human mind can be absolute chaos. Through these objectives, we have observed the complex nature of even one single moment. And it's a lot of activity. This chaos can seep into our lives and tire us out, sometimes at the worst possible moment.

For example

You have an exam coming up, and it's a subject that you absolutely detest. You have plenty to study, and since you don't enjoy the subject, you're easily distracted. The closer the exam gets, the tenser you get. You feel anxious and unprepared. You aren't sleeping too well. You keep thinking of the exam or the consequences of not doing well. That's a lot to experience, especially with a difficult exam around the corner.

$$(a + b)^3 = a^3 + 3a^2b + 3ab^2 + b^3$$

Practicing mindful breathing, thought defusion, or tuning into your emotions can really help. It can help untangle the chaos after which, you'll manage your time better and be less anxious about giving the exam.

Any time you start feeling overwhelmed, just take a few moments for yourself and do these exercises. You can use mindful breathing to calm down and tune into your emotion to reduce its intensity.

Objective completed. Don't forget to fill in the triangle.

Congratulations, friend! You've successfully completed all the objectives at Mindful Mountain. Please proceed to collect your certificate and reward.

This is to certify that

_____

has completed the quest:

'Discover your inner focus'

at Mindfulness Mountain

on_____

G Dave

Signed

Guru Dave

Mindfulness Mountain is a challenging course. Many people don't make it past the first or second objective. But you did. You survived, and so, as a reward, I shall teach you a secret skill that you can use for life— The Wise Mind.

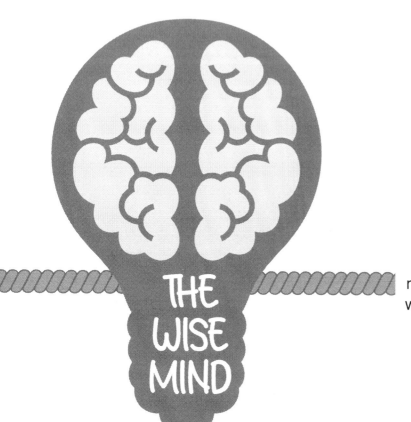

All of us have two minds, an emotional mind, and a reasonable mind. Most decisions we make will feel like a tug of war between these two minds.

For example

You're going to meet a friend after a really long time. You've planned something really special that you've been discussing for weeks. But, on that day, your friend's family member falls ill. Your friend calls you and cancels at the last minute.

You feel very upset because you were really looking forward to it. But you know that logically, your friend couldn't have abandoned their family member. Your friend didn't cancel the plan to hurt you in any way. Despite being aware of this, you still feel upset. This is because of your emotional mind.

THE REASONABLE MIND

Cool, rational, listens to facts, and is constantly trying to solve problems.

When the reasonable mind is in control, values and feelings are secondary.

THE WISE MIND

Both of these minds co-exist.

It brings out wisdom in you by acknowledging your emotions and being logical at the same time.

THE EMOTIONAL MIND

Hot, variable, and listens to feelings.

When the emotional mind is in control, facts and reasoning are secondary.

As you grow older, you'll find yourself in situations where you'll choose to lean on your reasonable mind rather than your emotional mind. You may go to bed early even though you want to stay up. You may skip going to a party because you have work or a chore to do.

Let's try accessing the Wise Mind Headquarters with a short meditation.

CONNECTING TO <u>WISE MIND</u> HEADQUARTERS

You will need:

▲ A timer
▲ A comfortable space where you won't be disturbed

Please read the instructions before you begin.

 Warning: This may feel weird.

Instructions

1. Set the timer for 3 minutes.

2. Close your eyes.

3. Place your hand on the center of your torso—between the end of your rib cage and your belly button. This is the location of your Wise Mind Headquarters [HQ].

WISE MIND HEADQUARTERS

4. Spend a little time focusing on your breathing.

5. Think of a problem that you've been having lately and focus on your HQ.

   What are the thoughts that come up? Observe them without engaging with them.

   Observe your emotions. What are the feelings associated with this problem?

6. Become aware of what your emotional mind and reasonable mind are saying. Let intuition guide you. A solution or multiple solutions will eventually take form, taking both minds into account.

7. Use the rest of the time to think about the solution(s).

8. When the timer goes off, open your eyes and return your focus to the room.

Does it really work?

Can it really be that simple? You just close your eyes, meditate, and the answers will come to you?

Well, yes and no. If you observe the exercise above, you'll notice that it's a combination of many of the exercises you completed at Mindfulness Mountain.

▲ Spend a little time focusing on your breathing. [Breathflix]
▲ What are the thoughts that come up? Observe them without engaging with them. [Thought Express Deactivation]
▲ Observe your emotions. What are the feelings associated with this problem? [The Emotion Station]

If you try to connect to the HQ before practicing these exercises, you may not see any results. But if you practice everything that you've learned at Mindfulness Mountain, it'll be easier for you to connect to the HQ. In time, making decisions using your wise mind will become a habit and come to you naturally.

PRACTICING DAILY MINDFULNESS

Remember, each and every skill you learn needs practice. Even if you've completed the workbook, you'll need to practice these things in your daily life. Here are some ways you can benefit from incorporating mindfulness into your everyday life:

Be as mindful as you can be

Doing everything mindfully can reduce the incidents we discussed earlier [like walking into a room and forgetting why you're there]. But, take it slow.

Start by mindfully doing small activities like brushing your teeth or tying your shoelaces. Think about what you're doing, how it makes your body feel, and any thoughts and emotions that come along with it.

Then, you can add activities like exercising, coloring, doodling, gardening, listening to music. It's easy to do these tasks mindfully because they are repetitive in nature.

Eventually, you can add chores which will help you become focused, efficient and swift at everything you do.

Calming down and relaxation

The most common use of mindfulness is to relax; when you're feeling overwhelmed or just want to wind down at the end of a stressful encounter or a long hard task.

Here are some ways you can use the activities that you learned:

▲ 'Under the scanner' can help you fall asleep.
▲ 'The emotion station' can help you calm down from intense emotions.
▲ Deep breathing can help you calm down when you're feeling anxious.

To get into the habit of practicing mindfulness, here's a 10-day challenge that you can do:

Mindful tasks and exercises completed
☐ Day 1
☐ Day 2
☐ Day 3
☐ Day 4
☐ Day 5
☐ Day 6
☐ Day 7
☐ Day 8
☐ Day 9
☐ Day 10

Well, friend, it is here that we part ways.

I hope you enjoyed your stay at Mindfulness Mountain and that you'll cherish the Wise Mind.

You can proceed to Distress Desert, where the Sgt. Dawson will guide you through your objectives.

I wish you all the best.

G Dave

QUEST 2

TRAIN IN DISTRESS ENDURANCE

Distress. We all experience it. There's no escaping it. It could be physical distress like pain from stubbing your toe, or emotional distress like the sadness that comes with grief and some unlucky times, both together.

It's unpredictable. A day may start off really well but go downhill with just one horrible incident (falling down, having a bad argument, or even unexpected rainfall). So much of what causes us distress isn't even in our control.

It's unpleasant. The thoughts and emotions we experience in distress are painful and last longer than we want them to. Sometimes the emotions are disproportionate to what happened and feel like a big overwhelming wave.

What's in it for you?

In the face of distress, we all have the urge to do something. It is natural to want to stop feeling the pain. The way we deal with distress is called a coping strategy. There's no class that teaches you this at school. Hence, many people tend to learn unhealthy or unhelpful coping strategies from their environment.

Let's look at some of these. Check the ones that you may have done in the past.

☐ Over-analyse the situation thoroughly

☐ Think of other situations where you felt the same

☐ Worry about it happening again in the future

☐ Doing things to avoid it in the future

☐ Isolating yourself from everyone

- ☐ Feeling irritable with your family and friends

- ☐ Punishing yourself by not eating or denying yourself something you like doing

- ☐ Hurting yourself in some way

- ☐ Turning to harmful habits

For example

Let's say you have a piano recital at school and you practice for weeks. On the day of the performance, you miss one note, and it makes a mess of your timing.

What are the emotions you feel? Embarrassment, sadness, and maybe a little bit of anger? You may use some of the ways we mentioned.

And while they help in the moment, they also have consequences that you probably haven't considered:

Coping strategy	Example	A possible consequence
Over-analyse the situation thoroughly	"Ugh, if only I hadn't got distracted. I should have done.... Or this...."	Keeps your mind on the incident and off other things that are actually going well for you.
Think of other situations where you felt the same	"This is exactly like that time I missed the goal."	Adds to the distress you're already feeling.
Worry about it happening again in the future	"What if I do it the next time as well?"	Miss the things that are going well for you right now.
Doing things to avoid it in the future	"I'm never playing the piano again."	Removes the opportunity to get better at it.

Isolating yourself from everyone	"I just want to be alone."	Spending time alone gives you more time to think about the distress and mull over it.
Feeling irritable with your family and friends	"Why won't everyone just leave me alone!"	Saying something in anger can harm the relationship.
Punishing yourself by not eating or denying yourself something you like doing	"I don't deserve to feel good."	It'll reinforce the idea that you deserve the distress and lead to unhealthy habits.
Hurting yourself in some way	"I deserve the pain."	It'll make you feel physically unwell and further the distress you're feeling.
Turning to harmful habits	"Eh, what's the point? I'm a failure."	It won't reduce your distress but instead, have other more harmful consequences.

So while you're trying to overcome the distressing situation, you may end up either making it harder for yourself or creating another distressing situation.

Try to think of a distressing situation in your life where you used these coping strategies.

Describe the situation and put down a consequence as well. You can also add other unhelpful coping strategies that you can think of.

Coping strategy	Example	A possible consequence
Over-analyse the situation thoroughly		
Think of other situations where you felt the same		

Worry about it happening
again in the future

Doing things to avoid it in the
future

Isolating yourself from
everyone

Feeling irritable with your
family and friends

Punishing yourself by not
eating or denying yourself
something you like doing

Hurting yourself in some way

Turning to harmful habits

Where do we learn these unhealthy strategies?

Well, we pick some of them up by watching people around us, and the others come to us naturally. But the good news is that we can replace them with new healthier, and effective ones. And that's what brings us to Distress Desert.

At ease, Cadet. I am Sergeant Dawson, and I'll be taking you through the Distress Desert. Your objective here is to complete training in three courses that'll train you in tactics you can use to endure distress. Find mission details attached. You'll be awarded a badge of honor and a highly confidential skill at the end of the courses. I wish you all the best for this quest.

Dismissed.

Sergeant Dawson

CLASSIFIED

DISTRESS DESERT

Train in
distress endurance
at Distress Desert

1. Create diversion

2. Collect yourself

3. Cope with it

Complete the courses in order.

Upon completion of the course, **do not forget to fill in the square**.

You need all three squares filled in to complete this quest and collect your reward.

MISSION #01-480

Mission: Distress endurance

Security level: Highly confidential

_____ Date

Distress is a recurring threat that cannot be destroyed. On most occasions, it comes around and leaves with minor damage. But sometimes, it creates mass hysteria among the public.

You, Cadet, are tasked with reducing its impact. You must follow protocol

Step 1: Create a diversion for civilians
Step 2: Collect yourself
Step 3: Confront the threat

At Distress Desert, you will be trained in these steps. You will also create customized strategies that highlight your strengths and skill set. Good luck.

Signed
Sergeant Dawson

Course 01: Create diversion

When you're in distress, your thoughts may constantly circle back to what's bothering you and keep you in a state of misery. You need to create a diversion to distract yourself from the cause of distress.

You've mastered the art of focus at the Mindfulness Mountain. Now you'll learn to create a diversion from the distress by channeling your focus on other things.

In this course, you have six tactics to learn:

- Proceed with caution
- Deploy gratification
- Offer assistance
- Transfer focus
- Evacuate
- Mundane task completion

At the end you will develop a strategy to create diversion.

Tactic 01: Proceed with caution

A lot of people tend to harm themselves or others when they feel overwhelmed by distress. This is due to the intensity of the emotion and feeling like they can't control it.

For example, when we're angry, we may physically feel the emotion—a rush of blood in our veins, or a feeling of warmth in our forehead. We may feel the urge to take it out on the person who's making us angry by yelling at them or striking them. We may say things we'll regret or get violent. This only escalates the situation and leads to even more distress.

Here are some things that you can do to safely vent out your emotions without running the risk of causing harm or ruining a relationship.

- Label a balloon with who or what you're angry with and pop it. If you don't like loud noises, write on a paper and scratch over it with a marker.

- Keep a private online journal. Write about how you're feeling. If you're upset with someone, write a letter to them pouring your heart out but don't send it.

Sergeant recommends: Penzu, monkkee, journey.cloud

- Scream into a pillow. Punch it or just whack one pillow with another.

- Just cry. Bottling it inside can add to the pressure. If you're unable to cry, watch a movie that never fails to make you cry.

- Physically exhaust yourself. Go for a run. Or put on some music and dance it out.

What are other safe methods that you can use to let go of an overwhelming emotion?

_____

_____

_____

Tactic 02: Deploy gratification

There's no better way to distract yourself than doing something that you enjoy. This could be an interest or hobby, or even just something you like to do for leisure. It helps to have a nice extensive list of things you can do to improve your mood.

Here are some of the things on my list:

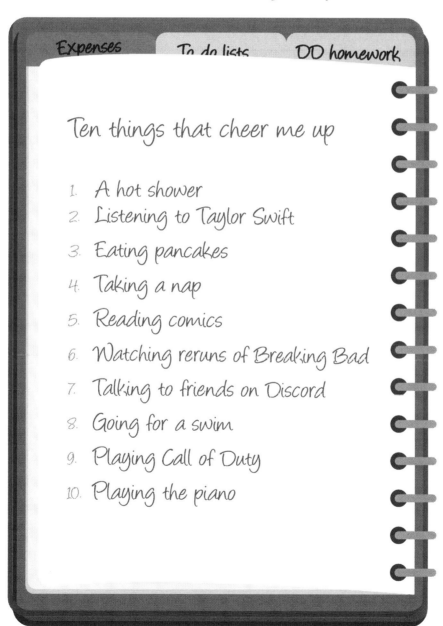

Expenses   To do lists   DO homework

Ten things that cheer me up

1. A hot shower
2. Listening to Taylor Swift
3. Eating pancakes
4. Taking a nap
5. Reading comics
6. Watching reruns of Breaking Bad
7. Talking to friends on Discord
8. Going for a swim
9. Playing Call of Duty
10. Playing the piano

For now, create a small list of things that cheer you up. At the end of the course, you'll have to make a list of one hundred things that cheer you up. I know it sounds like a lot, but once you get started, you'll realize that there are indeed more than a hundred things that can cheer you up.

Ten things that cheer me up

1.

2.

3.

4.

5.

6.

7.

8.

9.

10.

Tactic 03: Comradery

One of the reasons that distress can be overwhelming is because you experience it on your own. You tend to feel alone in your thoughts, emotions, and overall experience. Changing that focus from within to someone else can distract you and make you feel better.

Here are some ways that you can distract yourself by thinking of others:

1. Do something for another person

This could be helping **someone you know** by running an errand for them, buying them something from the supermarket, or raking the leaves in their yard. Ask your family and friends if there's something you can do for them.

It could be **someone you don't know**. You could volunteer at a local shelter or soup kitchen. If you like spending time with animals, you could even volunteer at an animal shelter.

It need not even be something they need help with. You could call a friend and just take them out for a meal. Or plan a surprise for a family member for no reason. The idea is to distract yourself by focusing your mind and energy on somebody else.

2. Just observe people

Go to a place with lots of people—the park, a skating rink, the mall. Just sit and watch the people walking by. Observe them, the way they dress, what they're doing, the conversations they're having. Imagine their lives; what brings them there? Imagine the relationship between two people; what would it be like?

You could even conduct a little survey of your own—like how many people are wearing pants and how many skirts? Count the number of people wearing glasses. Count the number of people wearing red.

3. Think of another person or pet

You could carry a photograph of someone you really care about and look at it when you feel distressed. Make an album on your phone of pictures of your pet that cheer you up, or just a collection of good memories with those whom you love.

You could even think about a person you admire, like a celebrity. Think of what you like about them or imagine a conversation that you'd have with them. If you're religious, think about God. If you're spiritual, think of the universe. Listen to how they would comfort you.

Do you have any other ideas of how you can distract yourself by thinking of others?

_____

_____

_____

Tactic 04: Divert focus

At Mindfulness Mountain, you got to observe the Thought Express. While it is quite hard to gain control over it, it can be used to divert focus away from the stress.

Let's do a small experiment, grab your timer.

Who's your favorite fictional character?

_____

Set the timer for one minute.

Now close your eyes and think about them—what do they look like? What do they sound like? Observe them until the timer rings.

Now set the timer for one minute again and close your eyes—only this time I want you to think about anything but the character you chose.

Try and block the character from your thoughts. Observe the number of times the character pops back into your mind.

Be honest. It was extremely hard to not think about it. And this is what happens to us when we're in distress. The harder we try to forget about what happened, the more we think of it.

So then, how does one use their thoughts as a distraction? You consciously divert your focus towards other things using mindfulness.

Here are some thoughts you could mindfully occupy your mind with:

1. A memory

Take your mind back to a memory that makes you feel good. For example, a holiday that you really enjoyed. Mindfully remember as many details as you can. Where did you go? Who was with you? What did you do there? Use your senses to immerse yourself in that memory. What did you see? What did you eat? How was the weather?

2. Observation

Look around, where are you? What's the weather like? What colors are the leaves on the trees? What are the people wearing outside? What are the sounds that you can hear?

Count things around you; stationary or moving objects. Count the number of things that are blue or the number of electric cars, depending on where you are. This is an easy way to distract yourself because you can do it anywhere, and you can do it differently each time.

3. Imagination

Think of a plot and play the lead role in it. It could be an ultra-cool fight scene from a movie that you really like.

It could even just be a fantasy of yours, like winning a Grammy or an Oscar. What would you say? What would your acceptance speech be like? What would you wear to the event?

Put on headphones and listen to a song you love and imagine yourself in its music video.

Recite your favorite prayer and feel the words cleansing you of your distress. Put on music that calms you and imagine a light washing the distress away or the distress being sucked out of you.

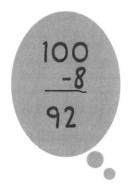

4. Doing math

Solving math problems takes a lot of focus. Don't open up a school book; we mean doing simple arithmetic in your head. For example, start at 100 and count backward by subtracting 8 each time. Or start at one and count by adding 13 each time. You can make your own rules and change them every time.

Remember that nobody can read your mind and see these thoughts. So, if some of these feel silly, it's okay; no one is ever going to know.

Make a list of things that you can use to divert focus.

_____

_____

_____

Tactic 05: Evacuate

Sometimes, the most effective thing you can do in a distressing event is leave. If you're in an overwhelming situation and you feel like your reaction is likely to make it worse, just leave.

For example, you're having an argument with a friend, and it's getting more and more heated by the minute. You're feeling extremely angry, and you think you might say something you'll regret. Excuse yourself and leave.

You can explain that you don't want to escalate the situation and need some time to compose yourself. When you're feeling calmer and the emotion's intensity has come down, you can resume the discussion.

Think of a situation where the best strategy would have been to leave. Describe it. If you didn't leave, what did you do? What consequences did it have?

_____

_____

_____

_____

_____

_____

_____

Tactic 06: Mundane task completion

Chores. Yes, groan, but chores can be used as a distraction too. Have you ever tried cleaning a stain when you're angry? It's incredibly fulfilling. When you use chores to cope with distress, not only do you feel better, but you also feel the satisfaction of completing a chore.

A helpful thing to do is to keep a list of chores. If you see a folder that needs sorting, add it to the list. When you're feeling distressed, you can look at this list and complete a chore.

Here are some examples of chores that you can do:

Sort out a drawer or closet

Clean up your email—delete old emails and trash

Organize the photos from your phone

Clean up your Downloads folder

Get rid of old things you don't need—clothes, books, shoes or gadgets that no longer work

Redecorate your room

Fix something that's broken

You're probably still not convinced about chores actually helping. But just try mindfully cleaning one window till it's sparkling the next time you're feeling outraged.

What are some chores that you have to do every week?

_____

_____

_____

_____

_____

Create diversion: a strategy

You've learned seven different tactics to distract yourself.

Experiment with them to see what works well for you. Observe them in different situations to see what works best.

Make a note of it and use it to make a customized distraction plan for yourself. A distraction plan is simply a manual to distract yourself from distress. You can print it out or save an online copy that you can easily access.

_____'s diversion plan

100 things that cheer me up	
1.	13.
2.	14.
3.	15.
4.	16.
5.	17.
6.	18.
7.	19.
8.	20.
9.	21.
10.	22.
11.	23.
12.	24.

25.

26.

27.

28.

29.

30.

31.

32.

33.

34.

35.

36.

37.

38.

39.

40.

41.

42.

43.

44.

45.

46.

47.

48.

49.

50.

51.

52.

53.

54.

55.

56.

57.

58.

59.

60.

61.

62.

63.

64.

65.

66.

67.

68.

69.

70.

71.

72.

73.

74.

75.

76.

77.

78.

79.

80.

81.

82.

83.

84.

85.

86.

87.

88.

89.

90.

91.

92.

93.

94.

95.

96.

97.

98.

99.

100.

List of chores I can do	
1.	6.
2.	7.
3.	8.
4.	9.
5.	10.

Other things that help	
1.	6.
2.	7.
3.	8.
4.	9.
5.	10.

How is this useful?

Distress can cause more distress. We've all seen it happen. A bad day just seems to get worse, and it feels like the universe is out to get us.

Diverting your thoughts or distracting yourself is an excellent way to make sure the distress doesn't multiply. Think of distress like a bug bite. The more you scratch and pick at it, the worse it gets. You need to leave it alone for it to heal; do anything but scratch it!

Similarly, distress can grow, escalate and expand if you feed more of your attention to it. The diversion plan that you've created can help in these situations and nip the distress in the bud.

Course completed. Don't forget to fill in the square.

Course 02: Collect yourself

Distress can also overwhelm us physically. When we feel upset, we may sob uncontrollably or we may tremble when we're afraid. To collect yourself means to calm down from that heightened state of emotion, so you can think and act with composure.

Mindfully immersing yourself by using your senses can help you calm down.

In this course, you will learn to collect yourself:

- With vision
- With sound
- With scent
- With touch
- With taste

At the end you will develop a strategy to collect yourself.

Tactic 01: With vision

Make an 'eye bleach' folder on your phone or PC and save things you like to look at. It could be things that you find cute, like cat GIFs or relaxing pictures of landscapes.

Hang a printout of a painting or picture that you really like on your wall.

Keep photographs of people or pets that you love and care about in your wallet.

Watch a movie with lovely cinematography and pleasant colors.

Make a playlist of your favorite music videos.

Make a list of things that you can do to collect yourself, using vision.

_____

_____

_____

Tactic 02: With sound

Make a playlist of songs that relax you and load it on your phone or PC.

Listen to a video of someone who has a relaxing voice explaining something mundane. You could also get an audiobook.

Listen to a podcast on a topic that isn't too serious.

Listen to the sounds outside—the call of the birds or the sound of a water hose.

Get an app that plays nature sounds. Explore them and bookmark the ones you find relaxing.

Sergeant recommends: Rainy mood, calm, Nature sounds

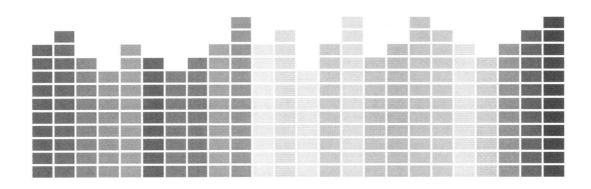

Make a list of things that you can do to collect yourself, using sound.

_____

_____

_____

Tactic 03: With scent

Smell a perfume you really like.

Go to a flower shop or a fruit stall and smell some flowers
that smell nice or fruits that you like.

Go to a bakery just to smell the aroma of freshly baked cookies.

Make a list of things that you can do to collect yourself, using scent.

_____

_____

_____

Tactic 04: With touch

Take a hot or cold shower, whichever you prefer.

Wrap yourself up in something soft, like an old t-shirt or a fleece blanket.

Play with a cat or dog with soft fur.

Sit on your favourite chair

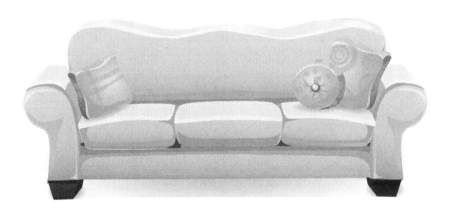

Make a list of things that you can do to collect yourself, using touch.

_____

_____

_____

Tactic 05: With taste

Mindfully eat something you really like:
Your favorite meal from a restaurant
A fruit that you like
Candy or chocolate of your preference
A home-cooked meal that you love

Make a list of things that you like to eat. You can use them to collect yourself, using taste.

Ten things I like to eat	
1.	6.
2.	7.
3.	8.
4.	9.
5.	10.

Collect yourself: a strategy

You've learned five different tactics to collect yourself. Experiment with them to see what works well for you. Make a note of it and use it to make a customized relaxation plan for yourself. A relaxation plan is simply a manual to calm down from the heightened state of emotion.

Make two plans, one for when you're at home and one for when you're away. There may be things that are relaxing that you may not be able to do at school or at a friend's house.

THINGS THAT CALM ME DOWN WHEN I'M AWAY FROM HOME

_____

_____

_____

_____

_____

_____

_____

_____

_____

THINGS THAT CALM ME DOWN WHEN I'M AT HOME

_____

_____

_____

_____

_____

_____

_____

How is this useful?

Distress can make you feel overwhelmed by emotion and hamper your ability to deal with the situation. You may be looking at the situation with cloudy lenses. Your perspective is blurred by the emotion and the accompanying thoughts and physical sensations.

Before you can address the situation, you need to clean those lenses. You need to calm down and compose yourself so your behavior isn't influenced by intense emotion.

Course completed. Don't forget to fill in the square.

Course 03: Cope with it

This course will teach you tactics that'll help you cope with the distress. You can either use them by themselves or combine them with the other skills you've learned.

What is coping? Coping is dealing with distress in a healthy and effective manner.

In this course, you will learn five tactics over two modules:

- Module 1: Coping for immediate relief
  - Safety reconstruction
  - Classical conditioning

- Module 2: Coping to prevent distress
  - Value restoration
  - Recess
  - Routine mindfulness

At the end you will develop a plan of action to cope with distress.

The tactics you'll learn in this course are slightly more complex than the ones you've learned before.

Good luck, Cadet.

Module 01:
Coping for immediate relief

Module 01 consists of tactics that offer immediate relief, as long as they've been rehearsed.

Tactic 01: Safety reconstruction

Safety reconstruction is an exercise that uses the memory of a safe place to get relief from the distress immediately.

You will need:

■ A comfortable space where you won't be disturbed

Please read the instructions before you begin.

Instructions

A safe space is a place where you feel safe and comfortable. It can be a memory, a physical location, an imaginary scene or anything that makes you feel safe.

What is your safe space?

_____

How do you feel when you're there? What about it makes you feel safe?

_____

_____

_____

1. Sit on a comfortable chair where your feet touch the ground. Put your bare feet flat on the floor and keep your hands rested.

2. Close your eyes and take a few deep breaths.

3. Imagine that you're in the safe space you mentioned and observe the place using all of your senses.

What does it look like? What time of the day is it? Is there someone else with you? Look at the things around you. If there's something around you that calms you down, spend more time looking at it.

What are the sounds that you can hear? Maybe some birds are calling? Perhaps you can hear somebody's voice. Observe the sounds and focus on those which soothe you.

 Now imagine what the place smells like. Is there a unique smell to it? Think of it. What's it like?

Imagine that you're touching the things around you. See how they feel against your skin.

 Lastly, use your sense of taste. Is there something you eat or drink when you're here? Recall it and observe the taste.

4. Now take it all in together. This is your safe space. Take as much time as you need.

5. When you're feeling calm or safe, take a few more deep breaths and open your eyes when you're ready.

Conclusion

By using all of your senses to imagine safety, you can actually convince your brain that you're safe, and it can turn down the intensity of the emotion. Once you've practiced the exercise a few times, you will be able to achieve a sense of safety much faster.

Tactic 02: Classical conditioning

You will need:

- A comfortable space where you won't be disturbed
- A watch

Please read the instructions before you begin.

Instructions

A cue word is the word you would like your brain to associate safety with. It can be anything you want—something you like to eat, a made up word, a fictional character, your favourite band—literally, anything.

Think of a cue word that you'd like to use to relax and note it down:

_____

Observe the time on the clock and note it down: _____

1. Sit on a comfortable chair where your feet touch the ground. Put your bare feet flat on the floor and keep your hands rested.

2. Close your eyes and take a few deep breaths.

3. Imagine that you're 'under the scanner' and the light is moving from head to toe, looking for tension that it can remove.

4. When you find a tense muscle, spend some time and imagine it getting relaxed, like the light is sucking the tension out of it.

5. Continue till you've scanned your entire body.

6. Now take a few deep breaths. When you inhale, think "breathe in," and when you exhale, think "(the cue word you chose)."

7. Do this for a few minutes.

8. Feel your body relaxing as you say the cue word. If your mind starts to wander, simply bring your focus back to the exercise.

9. When you feel calm or relaxed, open your eyes.

Observe the time on the clock and note it down: _____

Practice this twice a day, using the same cue word, until the time it takes for you to relax comes down. You may need to imagine the scanner at first, but eventually, you will be able to relax without it.

Conclusion

Have you heard of Pavlov's dogs, who were trained to salivate at the sound of a bell? Well, that's what we're trying to achieve here. We're training our brains to associate the cue word with a sense of safety. So when you're in distress, you can use the word to calm down.

Module 02:
Coping to prevent distress

Module 02 consists of tactics that you can use to prevent situations of distress.

Tactic 01: Value restoration

This tactic includes making a commitment to improving or maintaining what you prioritize in life. This can help you maintain a quality of life that does not cause distress.

First, you need to identify what you value in life. What do you consider more important than others, and what do you want to focus most of your energy on?

1. Rate the following aspects of your life, 0 being unimportant and 10 being very important. You can add any aspects we've missed out.

Aspect of life	Not important			Somewhat important			Very important		
Family:	0	1	2	3	4	5	6	7	8	9	10
Friends:	0	1	2	3	4	5	6	7	8	9	10
School:	0	1	2	3	4	5	6	7	8	9	10
Work:	0	1	2	3	4	5	6	7	8	9	10
Hobbies:	0	1	2	3	4	5	6	7	8	9	10
Having fun:	0	1	2	3	4	5	6	7	8	9	10
Religion:	0	1	2	3	4	5	6	7	8	9	10
Social beliefs:	0	1	2	3	4	5	6	7	8	9	10
	0	1	2	3	4	5	6	7	8	9	10
	0	1	2	3	4	5	6	7	8	9	10
	0	1	2	3	4	5	6	7	8	9	10

2. List out the aspects of life that you've given the highest importance to [rated between 5-10].

_____

_____

3. Now, for each aspect, make a plan. Your plan should have

■ A vision: A description of what you want that aspect of life to be like
■ Three action items: Things you can do to achieve the vision
■ A deadline: A date by which you want to achieve the vision

Keep it simple. Here's one I made recently:

I value	My health
I would like	to be able to run the marathon in six months
For this I'm willing to:	
1.	Give up junk food
2.	Work-out for 45 minutes every day
3.	Do deep breathing exercises
I will accomplish this by	<Marathon date> [Date]

4. Make three plans for yourself.

Plan 1	
I value	
I would like	

	For this I'm willing to:
1.	
2.	
3.	
I will accomplish this by	

	Plan 2
I value	
I would like	

	For this I'm willing to:
1.	
2.	
3.	
I will accomplish this by	

Plan 3	
I value	
I would like	
For this I'm willing to:	
1.	
2.	
3.	
I will accomplish this by	

Conclusion

Distress occurs when something you care about changes or gets disturbed. Identifying what that is and working to improve it can help reduce the possibility of distress.

These efforts will also enhance the quality of your life by reducing the gap between your current situation and your ideal situation.

Tactic 02: Recess

Recess isn't just at school. The brain and body require some time off now and then so they can function properly. And when we don't get the rest we need, we're more likely to get distressed, both mentally and physically.

When you're planning your schedule, always make room for rest. While you need to work hard at school or practice music or sports, you also need to take breaks. Without breaks, you will slow down, start to make mistakes, or end up feeling burnt out.

You can include recess in your routine by doing things that relax you like watching something, listening to music, reading, playing games or even just taking a nap. How can you include recess into your schedule?

Things I can do to take a break

Tactic 03: Routine mindfulness

Remember the techniques you learned at Mindfulness Mountain? Well, those magical techniques can help you prevent distress by keeping you in the 'now'. Our mind has the tendency to keep jumping across the timeline—sometimes bringing up embarrassing memories from the past or keeping us occupied with thoughts of the future. Both of these can cause feelings of distress.

Practicing the exercises you learned at Mindfulness Mountain can help you focus on what's happening right now. When you feel your thoughts following the past or the future, you can do the exercises to bring the focus back to now.

The exercises Inside Out and Breathflix are particularly effective.

Cope with it: plan of action

You've learned five different tactics to cope with distress. Experiment with them to see what works well for you. Make a note of it and use it to make a customized coping plan for yourself. A coping plan is simply a manual to manage your emotions when you're in a state of distress and reduce their impact.

Make two plans, one for when you're alone and one for when you're with other people.

For example, it may be easier to do Safety reconstruction at home; but practicing and perfecting Classical conditioning can help you cope when you're around others as well.

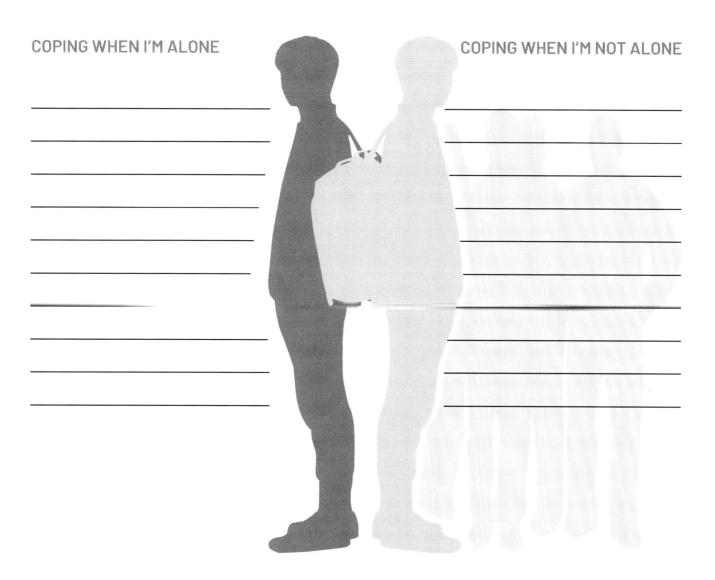

COPING WHEN I'M ALONE

_____
_____
_____
_____
_____
_____
_____
_____

COPING WHEN I'M NOT ALONE

_____
_____
_____
_____
_____
_____
_____
_____

How is this useful?

The earlier courses taught you to distract and compose yourself. Those strategies can be implemented immediately and bring down levels of distress while it is happening. Coping strategies, however, are investments that you make to reduce distress in the future. Even the first module's strategies require you to practice the exercise for the tactic to be useful.

For example

You have the flu, and it's the second time you've caught it in three months. The doctor prescribes you antibiotics to treat the flu. He also prescribes some vitamins to improve your immunity so you don't catch the flu easily.

Similarly, distracting and collecting yourself helps deal with distress immediately. But using coping strategies can help remove the possibility of distress in the future. You're addressing distress in a wholesome manner by confronting it at the moment but also preventing future instances.

Course completed. Don't forget to fill in the square.

Train in
distress endurance
at Distress Desert

1. Create diversion

2. Collect yourself

3. Cope with it

Excellent, Cadet. I knew you would ace the courses.
As promised, your reward awaits you.

This is to certify that

_____

has completed the quest:

'Train in distress endurance'

at Distress Desert

on_____

Signed

Sgt. Dawson

Distress Desert puts up a tough challenge, and you're still standing at the end of it! Marvelous.

As a reward, I shall teach you a top-secret skill—Radical Acceptance.

RADICAL ACCEPTANCE

Radical acceptance is finding the balance between:

- Accepting what has happened to you
- Changing what's in your control.

What makes it radical is that you accept the situation completely. You don't fight it or hurry yourself out of it. You understand the chain of events that has led up to this situation and acknowledge that while it makes you feel bad, you can do nothing to change what has already happened.

However, recognizing the role that you've played in the chain of events can help you make changes to your own behavior to prevent it from happening again. Radical acceptance is finding the balance between accepting what has happened to you and changing what's in your control.

Radical acceptance in a situation

You and a friend have a fight at school. When you get home, you're still seething with anger so you decide to vent it all out on social media. Your friend reads what you wrote and vengefully spills one of your secrets. The situation continues to escalate, and in the end, you both end up in detention with one less friend.

To apply radical acceptance, we would ask ourselves:

what were the chain of events that led to the situation?

What role did everyone involved play?

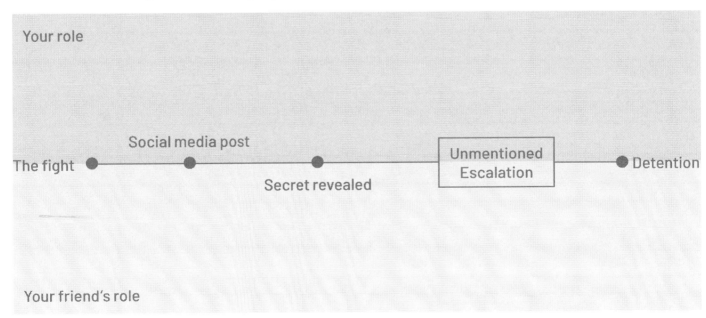

105

What were the consequences?

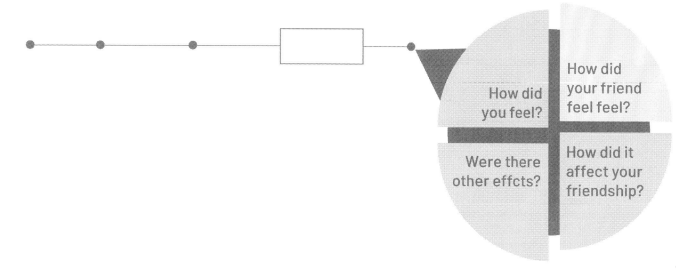

What could you have done differently?

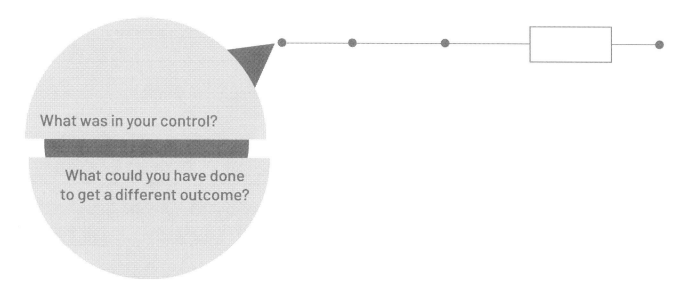

We use the first three questions to understand that situation is a result of a long chain of events that we played a role in. We accept that it has happened. We use the last question to gain an insight into how to avoid this situation in the future.

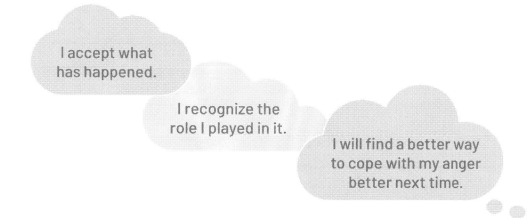

Now try and apply this to a distressing situation that you went through recently.

Describe the situation

_____

_____

_____

What were the chain of events that led to the situation?

What role did everyone involved play?

What were the consequences?

What could you have done differently?

Radical acceptance in yourself

Radical acceptance is a lens you can use to see the world and yourself. You accept those things that you cannot control and change those that you can. Not only can it help with distress, but it can also help you love yourself.

For example

"I'm not a very organized person. Even though I keep my quarters neat and tidy, my drawers are a challenge to keep clean back home. I end up using it as temporary storage for anything and everything. So what did I do? I created a little corner just for that. Once or twice a week, I sort this little corner and put things back to where they belong."

- Sgt. Dawson

None of us are perfect, and as we go through life, we find ways to make things easier for ourselves. Sergeant Dawson could get organized, but he couldn't stay organized, so he came up with his own hack. But to do that, he had to first accept that he was not an organized person despite being in the military.

Radical acceptance can help us understand our limitations, change what we can, and accept the rest.

Applying radical acceptance in daily life

Remember the thoughts we first discussed when you arrived at Distress Desert? How, when you goofed up at the piano recital, you thought you'd never want to play the piano again?

These are the kind of thoughts that naturally creep into our minds. However, we change them by using radical acceptance. Here are some thoughts that use radical acceptance:

Radical acceptance in a situation	Radical acceptance In yourself
This, too, shall pass.	I made a mistake.
This is only temporary.	I don't need to be perfect.
The circumstances aren't pleasant.	I'm doing the best I can.
These feelings won't kill me.	I'm not defined by my mistakes.
It is natural for me to feel this way.	I am good at some things, and I'm working on the others.
I'm just feeling _____ right now.	My experience of the world is my own.
It is what it is.	I take responsibility for my actions.

Here are some examples of how to use them in distressing situations:

Distressing thought	Coping thought
I had a difficult math exam and got a bad grade.	I'm not very good at math; I need to work hard. I'll do better next time.
Somebody called me names in a video game.	I feel angry, but I don't know this person, so it doesn't matter what they say or think.
Somebody made fun of what I was wearing.	I can't please everyone. I like it, and that's all that matters.
I lent my sibling something, and they lost it.	I feel bad, but there's nothing that can be done. This feeling will pass.

I had a bad argument on social media.	I'm a little agitated, but I'll feel better in some time
I feel upset after watching a sad movie.	It's natural to feel sad, and it'll go away.
My parents are having a massive fight while I'm in my room.	It's not a great situation, but it'll pass. I'm safe in my room and I'll be okay.

Think of three distressing situations from your past and a coping thought that you could've used.

Distressing situation	Coping thought

Remember that radical acceptance doesn't mean you accept bad behavior. There may be situations where you do nothing wrong and things still turn out horribly. These are difficult situations to cope with. However, understanding that you can't change what has happened can clear your mind and help you address the situation.

For example

If someone is cyberbullying you, you can use radical acceptance to accept that you're feeling very hurt. But, you can also channel your focus into doing what needs to be done, like filing a cyber complaint or bringing it up with your school authorities.

All right, Cadet. This is where I bid you goodbye. It's been fun, and I gotta say you're one of the finest I've trained.

I hope you'll use Radical Acceptance wisely. Now go on over to Emotion Island, where ~~Captain~~ the retired Captain will guide you. Good luck!

Sergeant Dawson

QUEST 3

SURF THE SEA
OF EMOTIONS

Anger. Happiness. Sadness. Guilt. Jealousy. Fear. Joy. Disgust. Enjoyment. Confusion. We're all familiar with these emotions and have experienced them at one point or another. While we may enjoy some of these emotions, the others can be pretty uncomfortable.

Emotions are signals that let us know how we're feeling in response to the environment around us. Our emotions help us survive, remember, make decisions and communicate.

Let's see how!

Survival

Before discovering fire or the wheel, we lived in the jungle, co-existing with predators of all kinds. When we encountered a large cat, a switch called the fight-or-flight response would get activated and give us a temporary upgrade. It would trigger a surge of alertness, focus, strength, and agility. It helped us make a run for it or fight the feline killer with poisoned arrows.

This switch still exists within us. Except, these days, it gets activated by a spider in the bathroom, an upcoming exam, or a piano recital.

Fear is what helps us survive whatever we think of as a threat. It helps us prepare for the worst and keeps us standing in the face of a challenge.

Memory

Imagine that a friend of yours from school moved away a few years ago and you haven't seen them since. They share a photo of the two of you on social media. It brings a smile to your face, and you feel happy remembering your times together.

That emotion you feel is how you felt when the photo was taken. Conversely, if you look at a picture of someone you fought with, you might feel anger or sadness remembering the fight.

Emotions help us remember past events and people because we make an association in our minds between the two.

Decision-making

Without emotions, we wouldn't be able to make any decisions. When you buy a muffin, how do you decide which flavor to get? You think of the flavors available and see what appeals to you the most.

Essentially, you are letting your feelings guide you towards the right choice of a muffin. Many of our choices throughout the day depend on how we feel—should I take a nap? Should I go see a friend? What should I wear today?

Communication

You get home from school and find a parent sitting at the table with their eyebrows furrowed. Your immediate thought is, "Whoops, what did I do!" They don't need to tell you that they're angry; you can read the expression on their face.

Similarly, you come home from a football game that you lost. Your parents don't need to ask you what happened because they can see the disappointment on your face.

Communication would suffer without emotion. No matter which part of the world you go to, pleasure is a smile, and pain is a scowl. Emotions help us understand each other.

What's in it for you?

Our emotions, thoughts, and behaviors can influence and be affected by each other.

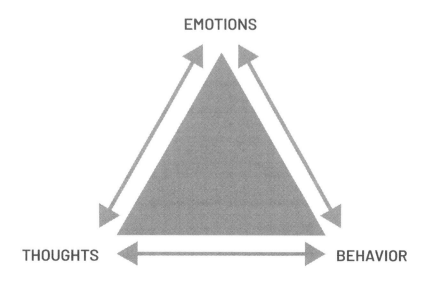

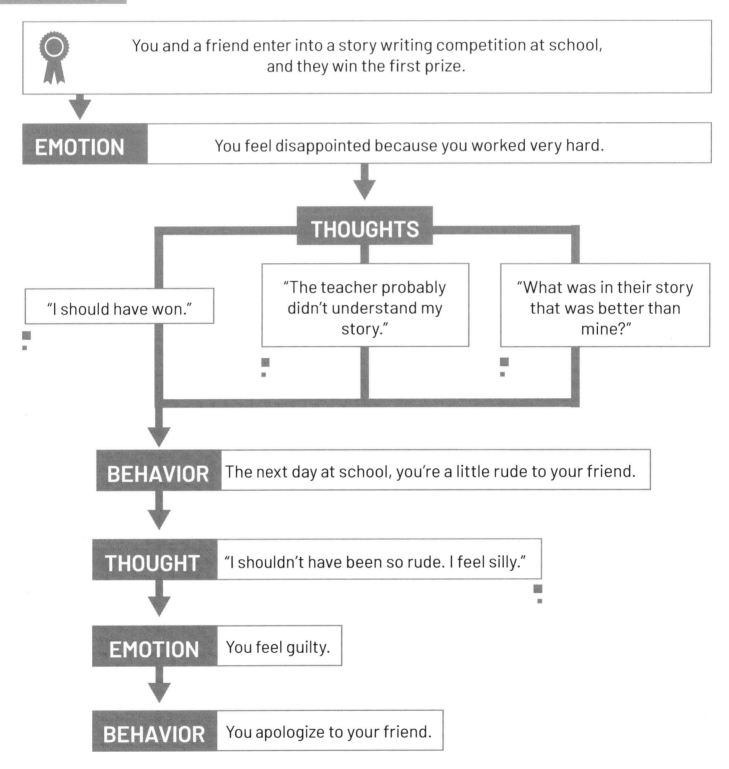

You and a friend enter into a story writing competition at school, and they win the first prize.

EMOTION — You feel disappointed because you worked very hard.

THOUGHTS

"I should have won."

"The teacher probably didn't understand my story."

"What was in their story that was better than mine?"

BEHAVIOR The next day at school, you're a little rude to your friend.

THOUGHT "I shouldn't have been so rude. I feel silly."

EMOTION You feel guilty.

BEHAVIOR You apologize to your friend.

This relationship between the three plays out in our lives all the time. We tend to overreact to things because we feel overwhelmed by the emotion. We say or do something out of anger that we don't mean. We aren't able to think of anything else.

Just like we can't control the Thought Express, we don't have complete control over how we feel. Our emotions are instant responses to situations. However, by developing a thorough understanding of our emotions, we can influence the thoughts and behavior that result from it.

117

On any given day, we experience a sea of emotions. They come and go in waves. Some are small and will hit the shoreline and dissipate quickly. Some build up before they come about and can feel like a tsunami. Welcome, friend, to Emotion Island, where we'll surf the sea of our emotions and learn to reign over them.

Turner

Retd. Captain D.B. Turner

Surf the sea of emotions at Emotion Island

1. Reading waves

2. The rocky shoreline

3. Lifejackets

4. Paddleboarding

5. Surfing

6. Swimming against the tide

Complete the chapters in order.

Upon completion of the chapter, **do not forget to fill in the star**.

You need all six stars filled in to complete this quest and collect your reward.

Reading waves

Before we deep dive into the vast ocean of our emotions, we'll learn to read the waves.

Chapter 1: Reading waves

At any given moment, we have a predominant emotion and secondary emotions lurking beneath the surface. To regulate our emotions and the intensity with which we feel them, we need to examine and correctly identify these emotions. We can do this by asking ourselves six questions.

Let me give you an example by answering them myself.

Reading waves

Describe the situation: My husband didn't attend my retirement party.

What led to the situation: I was rude to him that morning.

Describe how you felt: I felt bad. I know I deserved it, but I also felt bad that he missed such an important event in my life.

List predominant and underlying emotions.

Predominant emotion: Anger
Underlying emotions: Sadness. Guilt.

What you felt like doing: I didn't feel like staying at my retirement party. I just wanted to go home and go to bed.

What you actually did: Nothing. I stayed at the party and went home late. I had to stay. My colleagues and friends were all there.

The consequences: My husband was distraught. He told me that if I had just called and apologized for being rude, he would've come to the party. He had his suit ready and was just waiting for me to call! In the end, he missed the party, and I didn't have fun.

At first, I could only feel the anger because I felt like my husband was being petty by not attending the party. But when I did the above exercise, I realized that, beneath that anger, I was also feeling sad and guilty. I was feeling guilty for not apologizing and upset because my husband missed my retirement party.

Here's a copy of the exercise worksheet. Complete the worksheet every day for a week by choosing situations that you had strong feelings about or just something that happened on that day. If you need help identifying the right word for the emotion, consult the emotion directory.

Describe the situation.

What led to the situation?

Describe how you felt.

Predominant emotion:

Underlying emotions:

What did you feel like doing?

What did you do?

What were the consequences?

Describe the situation.

What led to the situation?

Describe how you felt.

Predominant emotion:

Underlying emotions:

What did you feel like doing?

What did you do?

What were the consequences?

Describe the situation.

What led to the situation?

Describe how you felt.

Predominant emotion:

Underlying emotions:

What did you feel like doing?

What did you do?

What were the consequences?

Describe the situation.

What led to the situation?

Describe how you felt.

Predominant emotion:

Underlying emotions:

What did you feel like doing?

What did you do?

What were the consequences?

Describe the situation.

What led to the situation?

Describe how you felt.

Predominant emotion:

Underlying emotions:

What did you feel like doing?

What did you do?

What were the consequences?

Describe the situation.

What led to the situation?

Describe how you felt.

Predominant emotion:

Underlying emotions:

What did you feel like doing?

What did you do?

What were the consequences?

Describe the situation.

What led to the situation?

Describe how you felt.

Predominant emotion:

Underlying emotions:

What did you feel like doing?

What did you do?

What were the consequences?

Now that you are in the habit of spending some time on your emotions every day, I want you to start observing them all the time and acknowledge how you're feeling by saying it out loud.

Yes, I know it sounds silly, but it can help take some of the power away from the emotion.

You don't have to yell it out or announce it; just a whisper under your breath is enough. At the end of the day, note the emotions you went through by using the worksheet below.

Do this for three days.

When and where?	How are/were you feeling?	Did you say it out loud?	What did you do after?

And that brings us to the end of this chapter. Yes, it wasn't much. Like I said, we're just dipping our toes!

How is this useful?

There are many advantages to correctly identifying how you're feeling.

Say you have a stomach ache, and go to the doctor. They run a bunch of tests to figure out what's wrong. It could be indigestion, food poisoning, acidity, or, God forbid, something serious. Once the doctor diagnoses it, they'll treat it correctly by giving you the proper medication or diet plan.

Similarly, identifying the right emotion can help you cope with it better.

Chapter completed. Don't forget to fill in the star.

The rocky shoreline

In our efforts to surf the sea of emotions,
we may stumble across some hurdles,
some rocks along the shoreline.

Chapter 2: The rocky shoreline

Most of the things we do are efforts to soothe ourselves or rid ourselves of an uncomfortable emotion (like anger, sadness, guilt, or confusion). We, as a species, crave to feel good and seek pleasure over pain.

But in the pursuit of pleasure, we also learn unhealthy ways to recover from uncomfortable emotions. It's because we associate emotions with certain myths. Let's look at a couple of myths in detail.

MYTH #1: THERE'S A RIGHT WAY TO FEEL IN EVERY SITUATION.

We may associate specific emotions with certain types of situations. A typical example of this is grief. When we see someone who has lost a loved one, we expect them to be sad, in tears, or upset. But people grieve differently. Some prefer to stay home and sleep the sadness away. Others want to spend time with their friends to take their minds off their loss. There's no one correct way to grieve.

There's no one way to feel about any situation. Emotions form your own unique experience of the world, and there's no right or wrong way to do that.

MYTH #2: NEGATIVE FEELINGS ARE BAD.

This is another common myth—experiencing a negative emotion is bad. We should avoid anger, sadness, guilt, or fear at all costs. Yes, some emotions don't feel good. But it's natural and healthy for us to feel them.

We make unhealthy connections between our emotions, thoughts, and behavior by avoiding a 'bad' emotion.

For example

* If you never allow a child to feel bad, they'll never learn to soothe themselves.

* If you constantly give in when someone throws a tantrum, they learn that they can always get what they want by screaming, skipping a meal, or locking themselves in their room.

Here's a list of other myths about emotions:

1. I shouldn't let other people know how I'm feeling; they may think I'm weak.

2. My friend thinks it's a silly reason to feel sad, so it must be stupid.

3. If it hurts, it's bad.

4. Intense and overwhelming emotions can help me be creative.

5. I'm just dramatic by nature!

6. I feel like they hate me, so it must be true.

7. Intense and overwhelming emotions are the only ways I feel motivated.

8. If I feel like doing something, I should be allowed to do it.

9. People who don't do what they feel like doing are not genuinely free.

10. Emotions are a waste of time.

11. Boys shouldn't cry.

12. Girls are emotionally weak.

Now, write a contradicting argument for each myth.

I shouldn't let other people know how I'm feeling; they may think I'm weak.

My friend thinks it's a silly reason to feel sad, so it must be stupid.

If it hurts, it's bad.

Intense and overwhelming emotions can help me be creative.

I'm just dramatic by nature!

I feel like they hate me, so it must be true.

Intense and overwhelming emotions are the only ways I feel motivated.

If I feel like doing something, I should be allowed to do it.

People who don't do what they feel like doing are not genuinely free.

Emotions are a waste of time.

Boys shouldn't cry.

Girls are emotionally weak.

Now think about situations where you used three of these statements or something similar. With them in mind, fill out the worksheet below. You can even try this with a couple of myths of your own.

Myth	Situation	What did you do?	What were the consequences?

Even after these exercises, you might catch yourself stumbling upon these rocks, and that's okay. Just make a mental note of it and do the above exercise when you have the time.

How is this useful?

Processing emotions is a task on its own; adding the burden of these myths only makes things harder. It's like carrying rocks in your school bag for no reason.

You may judge yourself too harshly based on how you feel, which you can't control. You may use them to excuse bad behavior, both yours and others. They can even influence your communication and affect relationships negatively.

Keeping an eye out for these myths and making a conscious effort to unlearn them can reduce the emotional burden.

Chapter completed. Don't forget to fill in the star.

Lifejackets

Before we set out to sea, we must put on our life jackets. They will help us surf the high waves with confidence.

Chapter 3: Life jackets

Our thoughts influence our emotions.

Remember this triangle?

What we think about a situation can shape the emotion we feel in response to it.

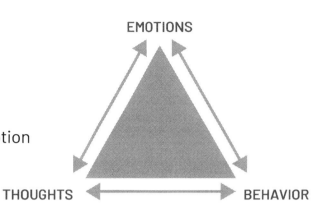

EMOTIONS

THOUGHTS ←→ BEHAVIOR

For example

My brother once sent me to pick up some butter so he could bake a cake. I went to the store, and instead of picking up plain unsalted butter, I bought a big slab of salted butter.

When I got home, my brother looked at the butter and asked,

> When's the last time you ate salty cake?

I felt like a complete idiot. The entire day, I was haunted by thoughts like:

> I'm a total moron.

> How could I be so stupid?

Hours later, these thoughts were still cropping up and making me feel ashamed and guilty. Even after the mistake was corrected and the cake was baked and eaten!

To this day, I still feel a pinch of shame when I think of that incident.

These thoughts are known as trigger thoughts, and we can get many of them in a day. Some people have them more often and find it hard to focus on anything, constantly being triggered to feel unwanted emotions.

Here are a few common trigger thoughts that people get:

1. I'm a moron.

2. I can't do anything right.

3. I'm a total failure.

4. Something's wrong with me.

5. No one cares about me.

6. Everyone always leaves.

7. I don't deserve to be happy.

You can challenge a trigger thought by using the coping thoughts you learned at Distress Desert (Page 111) or you can use a lifejacket.

Cruising

You will need:

⭐ A timer
⭐ A comfortable space where you won't be disturbed

Please read the instructions before you begin. This exercise is similar to Thought Express Deactivation. However, in addition to observing your thoughts, you will also be observing your emotions.

⚠️ *Warning: This may feel odd.*

Instructions

1. Set the timer for 3-5 minutes.

2. Take a few deep breaths and close your eyes.

3. Picture yourself in one of these scenarios:

You're lying on the ground and watching the clouds go by

You're driving down a highway, and billboards are going by

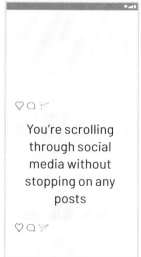

You're scrolling through social media without stopping on any posts

You're watching the end credits of a movie

In whichever scenario you choose, see your thoughts and emotions go by (on the clouds, billboards, posts, or written as credits) and keep breathing.

Use Radical Acceptance while doing this. Don't judge the thoughts and emotions. Don't try to stop or pause at any of them; just let them go by.

Let them appear in the form in which you think of them - a picture, a moving image, a word, or sentence. If many thoughts and emotions appear simultaneously, let them all rise and decline together. If a thought about this exercise crosses your mind, let that go too.

If you find yourself holding onto a thought or emotion, just consciously detach yourself and let it go.

4. When the alarm goes off, slowly open your eyes and return your focus to where you are.

Conclusion

This exercise, known as thought-and-emotion defusion, helps us stop going down the spiral of a trigger thought. It allows us to simply cruise through our thoughts and emotions without engaging with them.

Rowing

When you row a boat, you use two oars—one on either side. Similarly, you can counter trigger thoughts by finding a balance between your thoughts and emotions. Look at the following situations:

You're generally an above-average student. You write a short essay for your Spanish test and get a C. You immediately feel like you're a loser and a failure.

Your best friend invites you to their birthday party at 4 pm. However, you've got basketball practice until 4:30 pm and can only be there by 5 pm. When you tell them this, they react by saying, "Am I not important to you? How can you abandon me on my birthday?"

The first time you went to see a concert with your friends, you came home really late. You never cross your curfew otherwise. But every time you bring up going out with your friends again, your parents remind you of that one time you stayed out late.

In each of these situations, someone is forming biased opinions or statements based on one incident.

- ★ You get one C and jump to the conclusion of being a loser.

- ★ Your best friend accuses you of abandoning them on their birthday, even though you're going to be only half an hour late.

- ★ You generally don't stay out beyond your curfew, and yet, your parents can only think of that one time you did.

This type of thinking is known as filtering. Filtering is when you don't consider the big picture and see only what confirms your trigger thought. It's like looking at the world with only one eye open.

Here's a worksheet that can help you see the big picture. Choose a trigger thought from the list and fill out the worksheet. I've filled out the first one as an example.

Try and do this for a couple of more trigger thoughts.

Seeing the bigger picture

Trigger thought: Nobody cares about me

Describe the situation in which you had the trigger thought.

When I'm feeling upset, I like to call my friends and talk to them. We are a group of five who have kept in touch for years. One evening, I was just feeling a bit low and decided to call them. Nobody picked up.

What were the thoughts you had and the emotions you felt?

Thoughts	I'm so alone. My friends have stopped caring about me. Nobody is there for me.
Emotions	Sadness, loneliness

What is the evidence *for* them?

Nobody answered the phone when I really needed them to

What is the evidence *against* them?

They're probably just busy.
They always called back.
Just because they're unable to talk now, it doesn't mean they don't care.

Describe the situation after seeing the big picture.

I feel bad that there is no one I can talk to right now, but it doesn't mean that nobody cares about me. While it helps to talk to them when I'm feeling low, I'll just have to do something else today.

How can you cope with the emotions?

I'm going to watch *Shrek*. It never fails to cheer me up. My friends may be free to talk after the movie.

Seeing the bigger picture

Trigger thought:

Describe the situation in which you had the trigger thought.

What were the thoughts you had and the emotions you felt?

Thoughts

Emotions

What is the evidence *for* them?

What is the evidence *against* them?

Describe the situation after seeing the big picture.

How can you cope with the emotions?

Seeing the bigger picture

Trigger thought:

Describe the situation in which you had the trigger thought.

What were the thoughts you had and the emotions you felt?

Thoughts	
Emotions	

What is the evidence *for* them?

What is the evidence *against* them?

Describe the situation after seeing the big picture.

How can you cope with the emotions?

Trigger thought:

Describe the situation in which you had the trigger thought.

What were the thoughts you had and the emotions you felt?

Thoughts	
Emotions	

What is the evidence *for* them?

What is the evidence *against* them?

Describe the situation after seeing the big picture.

How can you cope with the emotions?

How is this useful?

Our experience can feel so complex and detailed that we sometimes forget to see the entire picture. Emotions and their supporting thoughts can make us feel like our perception is the truth.

For example

You're hanging out with your friends, and you mispronounce the word 'Lieutenant.' They laugh a little and then correct you. You feel embarrassed. Later that night, while you're brushing your teeth, you're still thinking about it. You're still as embarrassed and think that they're probably thinking of your little goof-up as well.

Let's zoom out.

Your friends are back at their homes, but their minds are occupied with other things—something happening in their house, their homework, or a goof-up of their own. But because the embarrassment keeps bringing up the incident in your head, you feel convinced that everyone else remembers it just as clearly and as often as you do.

Seeing the bigger picture is essentially zooming out of that complex experience in your mind and realizing that your perception isn't reality.

Chapter completed. Don't forget to fill in the star.

Paddleboarding

Now that you're a little more familiar with being out in the sea of emotions, let's try a little paddleboarding.

Chapter 4: Paddleboarding

About 10 mins

You will need:

★ A comfortable space where you won't be disturbed

Please read the instructions before you begin. This is another defusion exercise like Thought Express Deactivation and Cruising. This time, you will be letting go of judgements as they take form in your thoughts.

 Warning: This may feel a bit ridiculous.

Instructions

1. Close your eyes and take a few deep breaths.

2. Think of an emotion. It could be one you're currently feeling, or you can visualize an event from your recent past and observe the resulting emotion.

3. Continue breathing and observe where in your body the emotion is coming from. Is it coming from your stomach? Your chest? Your head?

4. Then, observe if you have any thoughts about the emotion. Are any of these thoughts judgments that you have about yourself or others?

5. Now, picture yourself in any one of these scenarios:

You're looking at a chatbox. Messages are coming in and disappearing after you've read them.

You're watching the end credits of a movie

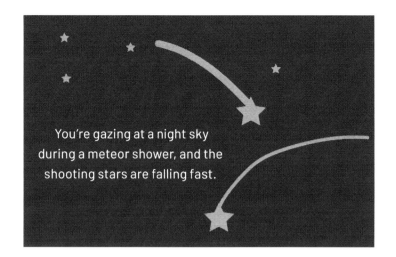

You're gazing at a night sky during a meteor shower, and the shooting stars are falling fast.

You're driving down a highway, and billboards are going by

Whichever scenario you choose, see those judgments come and go (on the video, billboards, as shooting stars, or disappearing messages).

Visualize the emotion like a wave. Observe how it rises and falls—paddleboard through the waves as they toss and turn.

Remind yourself that it's okay to feel the way you do. No matter how painful the emotion is, it's okay to feel it. Accept the feeling as a natural part of you that will go away. Continue to let go of the passing judgments.

6. Finish the exercise with a few minutes of mindful breathing by counting your breaths.

7. When you're done, open your eyes and return your focus to where you are.

Conclusion

This exercise urges you to be mindful of your emotions without judging them. It might feel strange at first because you may be used to criticizing your emotions. But practicing this exercise a few times can help you become less critical of yourself and more accepting of your emotions.

How is this useful?

Imagine that you're out shopping for some clothes. You see some shirts hanging on a rack. Some of the shirts look nice—you like the color or the pattern. The others aren't that great, and you may think they're ugly.

We tend to judge. We judge clothes, movies, games, music, shoes, and so much more. In these cases, judgments are harmless; they're just opinions that don't harm anybody.

But judgements about people can influence our behavior towards them. Similarly, we must be careful about judging ourselves based on our emotions. Emotions are impulsive signals. Being critical of ourselves based on them may lead us to set unrealistic expectations for ourselves (in order to prove them wrong). We may also believe the disheartening and hurtful thoughts that come with the emotions.

Practicing this exercise can help create a more encouraging atmosphere in our minds that is free of judgment.

Chapter completed. Don't forget to fill in the star.

Surfing

And here we are,
finally ready to surf the waves.

Chapter 5: Surfing

Sometimes, we're afraid to feel a certain way. We may avoid becoming close to someone because we fear they might abandon us someday. We become fearful of experiencing pain. We may avoid doing certain things or try to suppress painful emotiong.

In this chapter, we'll confront these emotions by figuring out how to cope with them in a healthy manner.

But first, we need to figure out which emotions we particularly dread. Fill out this record for a few days so we can identify the emotions that you feel uncomfortable experiencing.

When	What happened?	How did you feel?	What did you do?

Now that you've maintained a record of your emotions for a few days, identify the ones that occur repeatedly, the ones you can't shake off easily or both. Write them down:

1

2

3

4

5

Now, let's hit those waves.

You will need:

★ A comfortable space where you won't be disturbed

Please read the instructions before you begin. This is an exposure exercise that is designed to help you become comfortable with an emotion.

Instructions

1. Close your eyes and take a few deep breaths.

2. Focus on your breathing and become mindful of your body.

   Observe high-tension areas like your shoulders, neck, and head. If you use the computer a lot, your lower back; if you play a lot of sports, your legs.

   Become aware of the physical sensations.

3. Next, choose an emotion from your list and focus on it. What emotion are you feeling? Name it.

How intense is it? Which part of the wave are you on—is it peaking high up or swooping down low?

Describe the emotion as well as you can.

4. Are there any other emotions? What are they? Observe them.

5. Are there any new emotions? Continue to be mindful of them—their quality, intensity, and position on the wave. Describe them as well as you can.

6. Notice the actions you want to take in response to the emotion. What do you feel like doing?

You may feel afraid or uncomfortable when you acknowledge the emotion. That's normal.

Just try and stay with it the best you can while describing it in different ways.

You'll come across many judgments—about yourself or others. Paddle through them and let them go.

7. Observe what it feels like to stay in the emotion—to just let it be without doing anything about it. If it changes, observe the new emotion.

   Remind yourself that:

   This will pass.

   It's just a temporary wave of emotion.

   Every emotion that has risen has fallen, and this will too.

8. Stay as long as you can with the emotion. When you feel like you're done, take a few deep breaths to relax. Open your eyes and return your focus to where you are.

Conclusion

This exercise, known as emotion exposure, is essentially riding the waves of your emotions. Start slow and do it for five minutes at first. The more you do it, the more comfortable you'll become with accepting your emotions. When you feel like you can, do it for more extended periods of time. Try to do the exercise with all the emotions that you listed, one by one.

How is this useful?

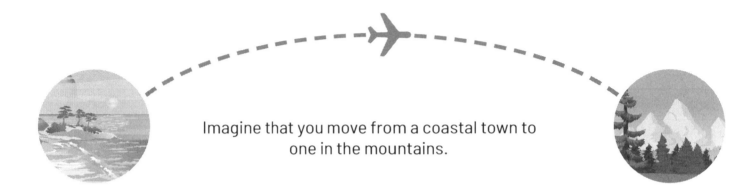

Imagine that you move from a coastal town to one in the mountains.

You're used to the warmth of the sun and find the cold in the mountains very harsh. The first year may be difficult as you're still adjusting to the change. However, in time, you adapt to the change and acclimatize to the new temperatures.

This is the objective of this exercise, but with emotions. When you're able to accept a difficult emotion and stay with it, coping with it will be less of a challenge.

Chapter completed. Don't forget to fill in the star.

Swimming against the tide

Chapter 6: Swimming against the tide

Emotions are a natural response. They aren't something we can control. They just happen. But, what we do with that emotion determines the consequences.

Acting impulsively on emotions like anger, fear or regret, can escalate the situation rather than alleviate it.

For example

You have a big test coming up. You start worrying about the test while you're studying. On the day of the test, you don't think you're going to be able to do well, so you fake a fever and stay in bed.

The next day your friends tell you it was the easiest test, and you could've easily nailed it. But your fear prevented you from even trying.

What do we do when we feel an intense wave building up within, and we can't find the privacy to do a mindful exercise?

We swim **against** the tide.

Swimming against the tide is doing the exact opposite of what your impulses are telling you to do.

Another example

You're at a cafe buying some milkshakes. The barista is being meticulous and cautious, and this is taking longer than expected.

Just as your patience runs out, the barista trips and the milkshakes fall to the ground.

You are livid.

You know that it was an honest mistake, but your anger is a 10/10. You want to scream; you want to ask for the manager, and you want the barista fired. These reactions are impulses that come with anger.

But, instead, what if you took a deep breath and politely asked the barista if they're okay? You acknowledge that the milkshakes are going to take longer. You have some time to kill; you can either give someone a call or mindlessly browse the internet without feeling guilty.
Eventually, your milkshakes arrive; the crisis that brought upon the anger ends, and you can get moving.

If you had screamed and asked for the manager, you probably would have had to stay much longer. Your anger would have continued to escalate rather than diminish.

Here are a few examples of swimming against the tide:

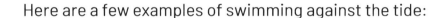

Emotion:	Anger	
Impulse action	**Swimming against the tide**	**Details**
Get rid of the anger	Validate the anger	"Yes, this is infuriating."
Attack	Avoid the situation	Leave and come back when you're calmer
Criticize	Radical acceptance	Understand that the circumstance is a result of a chain of events
Shout	Be gentle	Take deep breaths and consciously soften your voice
Cause harm	Distract yourself	Take a break and change your focus to something else

Emotion:	Fear	
Impulse action	**Swimming against the tide**	**Details**
Get rid of the fear	Validate the fear	"Okay, I am feeling afraid."
Stay away	Confront	Approach what you fear
Stop	Continue	Continue what you're doing even though you're afraid
Run away or avoid it	Face the fear	Get it over with
Cower	Stand up against it	Stand tall; make yourself bigger; let your body reflect courage

Emotion:	Sadness	
Impulse action	**Swimming against the tide**	**Details**
Get rid of the sadness	Validate the sadness	"I feel blue."
Isolate	Find company	Meet a friend; help a parent in the kitchen; hang out with your pet
Stay in bed	Get moving	Go for a run; put on music and dance, move around
Don't feel like doing anything	Do something	Do a chore; pull out your planner and set some goals
Slouch	Feel tall	Stand straight; stretch;

Swimming against the tide isn't just about doing the opposite thing. It's also about being the opposite—it's about standing tall when you're afraid—you must also alter your physical body to reflect the opposite emotion or action.

But aren't you faking it? Isn't that like blocking or suppressing your emotions?

Swimming against the tide doesn't mean we are in denial of a terrible situation and the discomfort or pain. We don't just put a smile on our faces.

We radically accept that something has made us angry, afraid, jealous, or upset, and we accept it. But we know that acting upon the impulse can make the situation worse. So, we swim against the tide as a response to de-escalate the situation and diminish the emotion.

We reign over the emotion.

How do we accomplish this? We answer six key questions.

Reigning over the emotion
What is the emotion I'm feeling?
I'm livid
Why do I need to de-escalate the situation or diminish the emotion?
I need to get my milkshake and leave. It'll just take longer if this situation gets escalated.
What is the emotion making my body do?
I'm frowning. My eyebrows are furrowed. I'm gritting my teeth. My breathing is heavy, and I can feel the anger in my bones.
What can I do to swim against the tide?
★ Acknowledge that I'm angry, and I'll calm down in a while.   ★ Be polite. Help the barista stand up; ask them if they're okay.   ★ Use a soft voice.   ★ Take deep breaths.   ★ Consciously calm my face.   ★ Distract myself with a game of chess on my phone.   ★ Call my friends and tell them I will be late.   ★ Watch cat GIFs.

Plan of action	
Validation:	I'm angry. The barista didn't do it on purpose. I have to wait a little longer.
Action:	Ask the barista if they're okay. Tell them to take their time. Take out my phone and play chess.
Body language:	Take a deep breath. Relax my face muscles. Use a soft voice.

After executing the plan of action

How am I feeling after swimming against the tide?

The anger disappeared faster than I thought, and the milkshakes were worth the wait. I feel all right.

Now think of three situations when you felt angry, afraid, and sad and fill out the worksheets:

Emotion:	**Anger**

Describe the situation.

What was the emotion you were feeling? (Consult the emotion directory to get the exact emotion)

Why did you need to de-escalate the situation or diminish the emotion?

What was the emotion making your body do?

What could you have done to swim against the tide?

What should have been your plan of action?

Validation:	
Action:	
Body language:	

Emotion: Fear

Describe the situation.

What was the emotion you were feeling? (Consult the emotion directory to get the exact emotion)

Why did you need to de-escalate the situation or diminish the emotion?

What was the emotion making your body do?

What could you have done to swim against the tide?

What should have been your plan of action?

Validation:	
Action:	
Body language:	

Emotion: Sadness

Describe the situation.

What was the emotion you were feeling? (Consult the emotion directory to get the exact emotion)

Why did you need to de-escalate the situation or diminish the emotion?

What was the emotion making your body do?

What could you have done to swim against the tide?

What should have been your plan of action?

Validation:	
Action:	
Body language:	

Now you're ready to swim against the tide. Apply this tactic over the next few weeks and fill out this worksheet every time you successfully swim against the tide.

Emotion	Impulse	Swimming against the tide	Consequence

How is this useful?

When you're learning to play the guitar, your fingers start to get a little raw. This can make practicing the guitar very painful. The only way for you to get rid of the pain is to continue to play the guitar. In time, your fingertips will harden, and you won't feel the pain.

Similarly, when it comes to controlling the impulses that come with our emotions, the logical thing is to do the exact opposite. Giving in to those impulses can make you say or do something you may regret, which can ruin your day and even fracture your relationships. And like all the other exercises, practicing this every time you get angry, afraid or disappointed, can help you get better at reigning over those emotions and recovering from them quickly.

Chapter completed. Don't forget to fill in the star.

Surf the sea of emotions at Emotion Island

1. Reading waves
2. The rocky shoreline
3. Lifejackets
4. Paddleboarding
5. Surfing
6. Swimming against the tide

Congratulations! You've completed all the chapters of the quest here at Emotion Island. Please proceed to collect your reward.

This is to certify that

_____

has completed the quest:

'Surf the sea of emotions'

at Emotion Island

on_____

Turner

Signed

Retd. Cpt. DB Turner

Now you're ready to reign over your emotions. A high wave of anger may surprise you when you're at the mall, but you'll ride it like a pro surfer.

However, this reward shall set you free from having to ride the big terrifying waves. I present you with my most precious discovery—Problem solving.

PROBLEM SOLVING

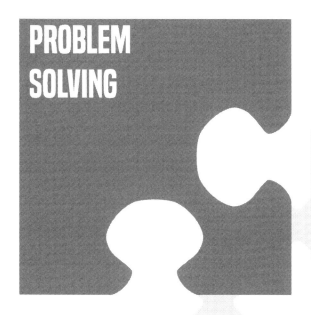

You can employ many hacks to control the emotion before it sends out signals of impulses and physical reactions.

Here are the ones that I have acquired and refined over the years. Since you've been such a keen listener and learner, I hand them over to you and trust that you will practice and value them.

Step 1: Inspect

We're all different, and our minds have their quirks and pet peeves. The things that can trigger those frequent recurring problematic emotions in our lives will be unique. Remember, there's no one way to feel in a situation.

Using this tool, you can identify your quirks and pet peeves and arrest that wave before it turns into an overwhelming tsunami.

For example

Every time I played a game with my friends and lost, I turned into a total baby. This made a lot of my friends and family not want to play games with me.

Inspection	
The behavior I want to change:	I'm a sore loser

What happened?

Situation:

We were playing Pictionary. I drew a gorilla, and my sister wasn't able to guess it. We lost the game.

Emotions:

Sadness, annoyance, shame

Thoughts:

"Oh no, we were so close."

Behavior:

I called my sister a moron.

Dig deeper by investigating your thoughts and emotions.	
Emotion	**Supporting thought**
1. Sadness	"We lost the game."
2. Annoyance	"Why is she so stupid?"
3. Shame	"I draw terribly."
What happened after?	
Everyone said I was immature and that this is why they hate playing games with me.	

The initial emotion that I had was sadness at losing the game. The annoyance and shame evolved from there. I made judgments about my sister, gave into my annoyance, and called her a moron.

Step 2: Make plan B

Now we'll develop a plan so that I'm not childish at my next Pictionary game.

Plan B		
Emotion	**Coping thought**	**Swimming against the tide**
1. Sadness	Remember that it's just a game. I can try and win the next game.	Congratulate the other team for winning.
2. Annoyance	Remember that we're playing the game to have fun, and I shouldn't take it so seriously.	Politely exclaim, "I can't believe you didn't get that! You named all the other monkeys!"
3. Shame	Remember that I don't have to be good at everything. My life doesn't depend on my drawing skills. It's no reason to feel embarrassed.	★ Laugh at my drawing of the gorilla and make fun of it. ★ Ask my sister how I should've drawn it so I can do better next time.

Shortlist the best ideas

Remember that it's just a game, and I shouldn't take it so seriously.
Congratulate the other team for winning.
Ask my sister how I should've drawn it.

Final plan

The next time I play Pictionary, I'll do my best to play for fun and not take it seriously. And if I lose, I will lose gracefully.

The next time I played Pictionary, I switched teams and still lost. I think my drawing skills aren't the best, but it's okay because the game was fun. I realized if I could just feel and confront the initial sadness that came with losing, I didn't have to resort to getting annoyed or feeling ashamed.

Try to think of a recent occurence of a behavior you would like to change and fill out the worksheet.

Step 1: Inspection

The behavior I want to change:

What happened?

Situation:

Emotions: Thoughts:

Behavior:

Dig deeper by investigating your thoughts and emotions.

Emotion	Supporting thought

What happened after?

Plan B		
Emotion	Coping thought	Swimming against the tide

Shortlist the best ideas

Final plan

You can do this exercise with recurring behaviors that you'd like to change.

Alas, my friend, the time has come for you to leave. I hope you enjoyed your stay at Emotion Island; I certainly had a great time with you. I wish you good luck for your last quest at Communication Caves, where Captcha awaits.

Take care, friend. Adios.

QUEST 4

MASTER
THE ART OF
CONVERSATION

Introduction|

Captcha v4.0

Welcome to communication caves, human.

I'm Captcha v4.0, and I'll be your guide for this quest.

I know what you're thinking.

"How can a machine teach me, a human, the art of conversation?"

I assure you, human, that I'm well-versed in the fine art of conversation.

As a machine, I'm constantly communicating.
You, too, do the same.

Input - You listen
Compute - You analyze, understand, empathize
Output - You speak

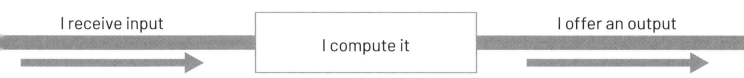

I receive input
I compute it
I offer an output

Humans seem to think that communicating and speaking are the same thing.

Communication includes input and output.

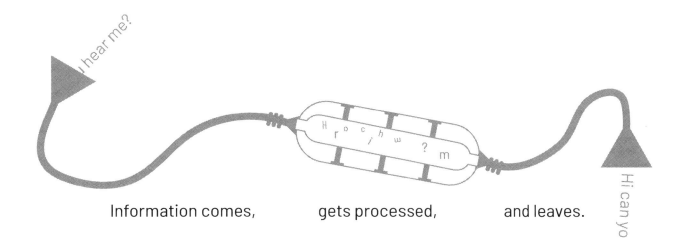

Information comes,   gets processed,   and leaves.

Even if you speak first, communication is complete only when the other person has understood you.

If there is a misunderstanding of your statement, communication has failed.

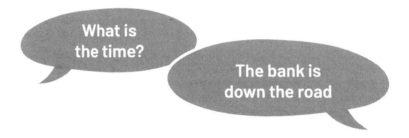

I will teach you all the stages of communication—input, compute and output.

What's in it for you?

Humans network. You depend on a network—of family, friends, teachers, classmates, teammates, colleagues, doctors, baristas, and even the teller at the checkout stand.

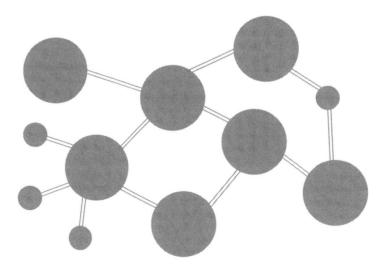

Your network is made up of relationships. The connection between two humans is what you call a 'relationship.'

Note: When I use the word 'relationship,' I'm referring to a relationship between any two humans, not just a romantic one. It could be a relationship with a close friend or the teller at the supermarket.

A relationship relies on communication to survive. Communication is the flow of information through the line connecting the two people.

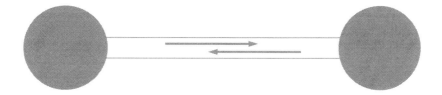

If communication breaks down, the connection gets damaged.

Repeated breakdowns can cause the connection to weaken and get severed.

This is how your relationships work. When those lines of communication are open and effective, the relationship thrives.

This quest is designed to teach you effective communication.

I'm told humans prefer to be referred to as persons and people, so I shall do the same.

Press ENTER to begin

Beep beep boop. Good luck.

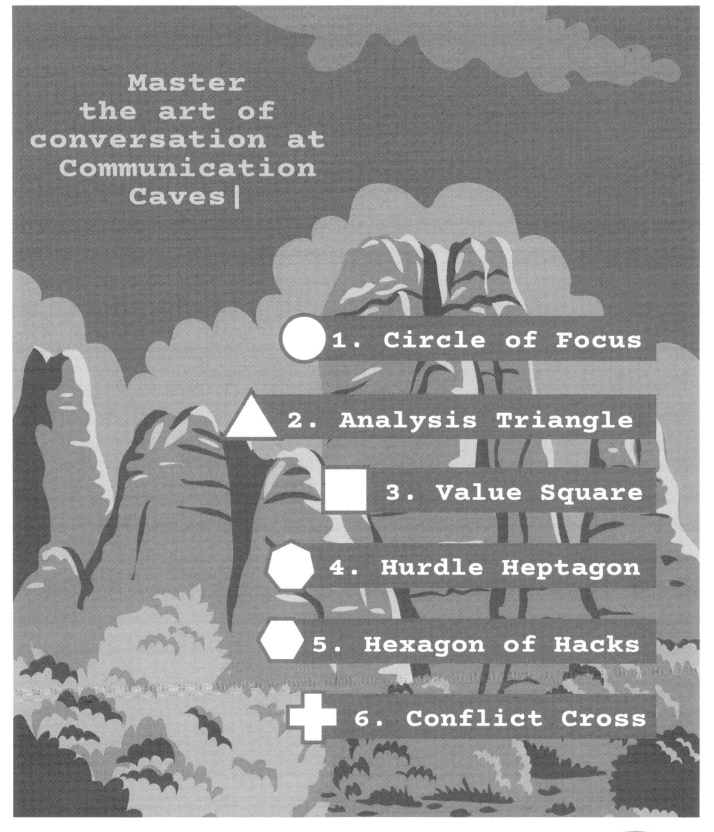

Master the art of conversation at Communication Caves|

1. Circle of Focus

2. Analysis Triangle

3. Value Square

4. Hurdle Heptagon

5. Hexagon of Hacks

6. Conflict Cross

Complete the caves in order.

Upon completion of the cave, **do not forget to fill in the shape**.

You need all six shapes filled in to complete this quest and collect your reward.

Circle of Focus|

Function: Learning to be mindful during a conversation.

Number of programs: 1

Welcome to the Circle of Focus.

First, a small exercise.

Have any of these happened to you during a conversation?

Check the ones that have happened to you!
☐   Your mind wanders off, so you don't know what they said.
☐   You're already cooking up a response while they're still talking.
☐   The other person gets angry or upset out of nowhere
☐   You realize both of you were making the same point in an argument.
☐   A calm discussion suddenly turns into an argument.

These situations occur when two humans people are having a conversation but not paying attention. The solution to this is to have mindful conversations.

Mindful conversations

Being mindful during a conversation ensures that the information being transmitted is accurate.

To do this, you should not only listen to what they're saying, but you should also observe what they're communicating without words:

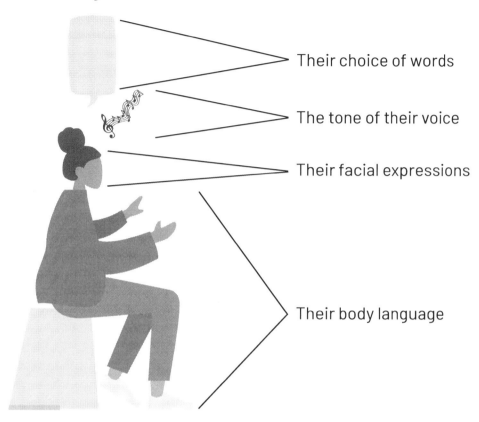

- Their choice of words
- The tone of their voice
- Their facial expressions
- Their body language

These pieces of information can help you gain insight into their emotions and responses. If, during a conversation, the other person's emotion shifts, you'll be able to observe it in their expression or tone.

For example

If a friend is getting irritated with what you're saying, they may start to sound sarcastic or use profanity.

You also have to be mindful of your own thoughts and emotions during a conversation. Mindful conversation also includes assessing comprehension:

Do you understand what they are saying?

Do they understand what you are saying?

Program 1: Cognizant transmission

The next time you talk to someone, have a mindful conversation.

Observe:

- The expressions on their face
- Their body language
- The tone of their voice
- The words that they're choosing to describe things

Be careful not to get lost while doing this and forget to listen to what they're saying. You need to notice all of these things *along* with what they're saying.

Additionally, observe your own reactions to what they're saying:

- How are you feeling? Is this conversation making you feel good or bad?
- Are they making sense to you? Do you have any doubts?
- Have they understood you properly? Is there anything you need to add to be more precise?

Again, remember to just observe your reactions and not get distracted by them.

Do you have a good idea of how they're feeling? Are there gaps in what you're sensing?

- If so, ask them questions to fill in the gaps.
- Are you all right?
- Is there anything you'd like to talk about?
- Do you understand what I'm saying?

Try and practice this exercise as often as you can. The more you do it, the easier it becomes, and eventually, it will come to you naturally.

Press Esc to exit Circle of Focus.

Cave completed. Don't forget to fill in the shape.

Esc

Analysis Triangle|

Function: To analyze your style of communication, needs, and beliefs

Number of programs: 3

Welcome to the Analysis Triangle.

Program 1: Operating system test

There are two extreme forms of behavior.

PASSIVE	AGGRESSIVE

Passive behavior is when a person compromises on things they want, in order to to keep relationships smooth. They may not express their emotions and needs because they want to avoid a conflict.

Aggressive behavior is when a person does whatever they can to fulfill their needs. They're generally described as bold, expressive, and those with a strict sense of principles.

Being passive may feel safer, but both of these have their own pitfalls. If you're more passive, you're likely to have lesser conflicts. But over time, you're likely to feel unhappy from always putting others first.

If you're more aggressive, you're likely to get what you want more often. However, you may go through more conflicts and push people away.

☐ I agree to do things even if I don't like doing them.

I make people do the right thing, even if they don't want to. ☐

☐ I'm chilled out regardless of what other people do or say.

I will speak up and tell someone off if they deserve it. ☐

☐ I'm sensitive to other people's needs and feelings.
It's okay if my needs aren't met.

I prioritize my needs and insist on getting what I want. ☐

☐ In cases of conflict, I compromise
and do whatever the other person wants to do.

If someone doesn't do the right thing,
I'll make sure they're punished for it. ☐

☐ I don't like upsetting anyone
and will walk away if I feel I'm going to.

I can't stand selfish people and I make sure
they know how they're behaving. ☐

☐ I leave people alone and let them be however they want.

If people are not being attentive, I will make them listen. ☐

If you chose more statements on the left, your communication style is more passive than aggressive. If you chose more statements on the right, your style is more aggressive. Enter your answer here:

My style is _____

Program 2: Need awareness test

Every person has their own needs. A need could be anything—companionship, personal space, or Chinese food that evening.

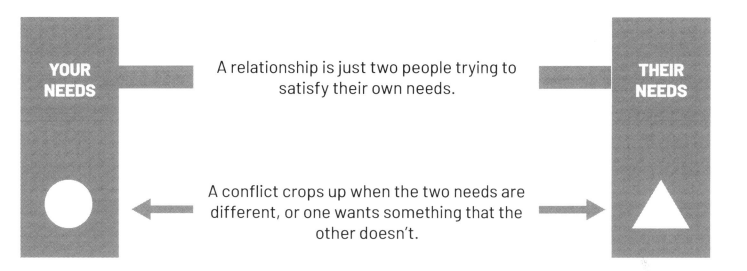

YOUR NEEDS

A relationship is just two people trying to satisfy their own needs.

A conflict crops up when the two needs are different, or one wants something that the other doesn't.

THEIR NEEDS

For a relationship to flourish, it is essential for a person to:

- Identify their own needs and express them
- Identify the other person's needs
- Negotiate to fulfill their needs
- Compromise to fulfill the other's needs

One person's needs being fulfilled more than another's can cause imbalance and damage the relationship.

Choose a relationship with a friend or a family member that you'd like to assess. List down your needs in the relationship and then jot down whether they're being met. Do the same for the other person.

For example

You need silence to concentrate on homework. But your sibling is making noise while playing a game. Here, the outcome is unsatisfactory. If they responded to your need by using headphones, the outcome would be satisfactory.

My wants	Outcome	Their wants	Outcome

Program 3: Connection prioritization test

You've already learned that there will be times when your needs will be at odds with the other person's needs. There will also be times when your needs will be put against what your relationship needs.

This is when you have the following thought:

I want to _____ but I should _____

You're not in the mood to go out anywhere. Your friend calls; their pet just died. Even though you want to stay at home, you go see your friend because it's the right thing to do.

But here, too, a **balance** must be achieved.

If you focus only on what you want, without caring about how it affects your relationship, you could damage it. But if you focus too much on what the relationship needs, you may sacrifice many of your needs and end up feeling resentful.

These are some beliefs or 'shoulds' which describe certain relationship needs.

Check the ones that you agree with.
☐ You should put your needs aside and tend to the other person's needs.
☐ If a person is hurting, you should do everything you can to make them feel better.
☐ You should show compassion all the time.
☐ If you know that the other person doesn't want to give something, you shouldn't ask for it.
☐ You should follow etiquette with people, even if that means you can't express your needs and feelings.
☐ You shouldn't decline or say no to someone; it isn't polite.
☐ You shouldn't express your feelings if it's going to upset someone.
☐ Other people's needs should always take priority over yours.
☐ You shouldn't hurt, offend or disappoint anyone.

If you checked many items, you have strong beliefs about following certain rules in a relationship. You may be putting the other person's needs ahead of yours to maintain the relationship. While it is admirable to have values, you should also acknowledge your own needs and ask for them in a relationship.

Your analysis is complete.

Press Esc to exit Analysis Triangle.

Cave completed. Don't forget to fill in the shape.

Esc

Value Square|

Welcome to Value Square.

What do you value in a relationship? Do you live up to your values? Reflecting on these aspects can improve your relationships, which can enable smooth communication.

First, make a list of things that you do that may be damaging your relationships.

What are things that you've done that belittle others? Or things you've done to hurt yourself or others? What are some values that you would like to uphold but you don't?

Here are a few examples from previous participants:

When my friends pick on someone, I join in.

I just can't keep a secret; I always tell somebody.

_____

_____

_____

_____

_____

_____

_____

_____

Now, make a list of values that you think two people in a relationship should uphold. It should be a list of rules of how you'd like to be treated or treat somebody else.

They shouldn't talk behind each other's backs.

They should always be honest with each other.

_____

_____

_____

_____

_____

_____

_____

Now compare the two lists. Are there things that you do that violate your own rules? Do you do them often? How do they affect your relationships?

Store these values in your memory; you'll need to access them later.

Press Esc to exit Value Square.

Cave completed. Don't forget to fill in the shape. ☐

Esc

Hurdle Heptagon|

(I didn't come up with the names, a ~~human~~ person did)

Function: To learn about the obstacles that interrupt effective communication

Number of programs: 7

Welcome to the Hurdle Heptagon

Before I teach you the hacks that will help you with your relationships, I must first prepare you for the obstacles you might face. There are seven types of hurdles.

Once you learn about an obstacle, see if you encounter it. And if you do, don't worry. Identifying the obstacle means you've won half the battle, and you can then learn to overcome it.

Program 1: Obsolete aggressive modes

When you get into a disagreement, you may use aggressive and unsympathetic ways to resolve the situation. These are known as aversive strategies.

For example

You go to a friend's house. You're in the mood to play a first-person shooter (FPS), but your friend wants to play a racing game. Chaos ensues.

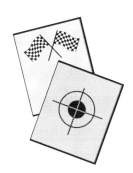

Aversive strategy	Example	The message it sends
Discounting	No, we're not playing a racing game.	Your friend's needs aren't important.
Leaving	Fine, I'm leaving.	If they want to spend time with you, it has to be your way.

198

Threatening	Put on the FPS, or I'm going to tell everyone that you're a _____.	They have to give in to what you want, or you will cause them emotional or physical pain.
Belittling	But racing is so easy; there's no challenge in it!	Their choice is silly or not good enough.
Blaming	You're the one who wants to play a racing game.	The conflict is entirely their fault, and only they can fix it by compromising.
Guilt-tripping	I would let you play whatever you want in my house.	They're doing something wrong by wanting to play a racing game.
Derailing	I don't care what you want; I'm feeling really bad now.	Your feelings are more important than their feelings.
Taking away	Fine, I'll never come to play here again.	Your need to play an FPS is more important than your relationship.

Many people use these strategies because they learn them from their environment while growing up.

Program 2: Obsolete passive modes

Similar to how people use aggressive ways to resolve conflict, they may use passive ones. In the same example, a passive response would've been to agree to play the racing game using the following thought processes:

1. They will feel bad if we play an FPS. I don't want to hurt them.

2. It's their house, after all; it would be rude to insist on playing an FPS.

3. I'll agree to the racing game. They may not want to be my friend if I don't.

4. It's okay; I don't want to argue.

You want to play an FPS, however, in each of the thought processes, you prioritize the following over what you want:

1. Their feelings

2. Etiquette

3. The relationship

4. The resolution of the conflict

While this will end the argument, using passive strategies frequently can leave you dissatisfied in a relationship.

Maintain the following log to see the strategies that you use to resolve a conflict. Are they aggressive or passive? Also, record the consequences of the strategy that you used. Did you get what you want? How did you feel about what happened?

When?	What did you want?	What did you do about it?	Were you passive or aggressive?	How did you feel about what happened?

Program 3: Emotion overload

Sometimes, during a conflict, you may feel overloaded by emotion. You may feel like you're no longer in control, and the reins are with your emotion. This kind of response generally leads to saying and doing things that you later regret.

When you are overloaded by an emotion, you may feel certain physical sensations or mental urges that you can't shake off. Making a note of these 'red flags' will help you address the situation before the emotion takes control. Here are a few examples of these sensations and urges:

Physical sensations
Warmth rising within your body
Racing heart
Trembling
Tension in jaws, forehead, neck, and shoulders
Breathlessness

Urges
To shout and scream
To strike someone or something
To dominate by winning or doing something better than the other person
To make them feel bad
To do something in revenge

All people have their red flags.

I feel the heat rising within me when I'm furious.

Think back to situations where you felt so overloaded by emotion that it took over. How did you feel physically? What kind of urges did you have?

Make a list of your red flags.

_____

_____

_____

_____

The aim of this exercise is to bring your attention to these red flags. When you feel them coming on, you can use any of the techniques you learned at Emotion Island to prevent the emotion from taking over.

Program 4: Need recognition failure

Communication skills become futile if you're unaware of what you need from a relationship. Sometimes you're aware of your needs but aren't able to convey them correctly. And sometimes, you haven't thought about it at all.

Think about the relationships in your life and what you need from them. List a few of those needs here:

Relationship	Needs

Program 5: What-ifs

A common hurdle to communication is worrying about possible responses that may be uncomfortable. What if they reject me? What if they get angry? What if they say no?

The fear of these 'what-ifs' can stop you from expressing yourself, and in some cases, make you avoid the situation altogether. Over time, it becomes an ineffective way to handle relationships.

In these situations, Wise Mind, the reward you received at Mindfulness Mountain, can help you assess the risk of going ahead with the communication.

Think of a situation where you'd like to communicate something but are afraid to. List down the 'what-ifs' and the evidence for and against them occurring. Also, rate the possibility of it happening.

What I want to say/do:

What if	It may happen because	It won't happen because	Likelihood of it happening (on a scale of 1-10)

Now choose the what-ifs that are likely to happen and write down how you can deal with them.

What if	What I can do

Using Wise Mind to tackle 'what ifs' can help you evaluate the risk and plan ahead. This way, even if what you predicted happens, you're prepared for it.

Program 6: 4 myths

One of the most common obstacles to effective communicationare myths that people believe about relationships:

1. It's wrong to want anything in a relationship.

2. Rejection, disappointment and anger are unbearable.

3. Saying no is not an option.

4. Nothing is in my control.

These four commonly believed myths can stop you from asking for what you need from other people or setting boundaries with them.

Let's dig deeper.

MYTH #1: IT IS WRONG TO WANT ANYTHING IN A RELATIONSHIP.

Humans are social animals, and as humans, you have needs. You need care, emotional support, love, and kindness. These are basic social needs and the reason why you depend on each other. Asking for what you need is essential and should be communicated.

THE REALITY: YOU HAVE THE RIGHT TO WANT THINGS.

 MYTH #2: REJECTION, DISAPPOINTMENT, AND ANGER ARE UNBEARABLE.

Yes, it is painful to be on the receiving end of rejection, disappointment, or anger. But it isn't something that you can't overcome. Think of the rejections you have lived through—yes, they were uncomfortable, but you survived. In the long run, you'll face more discomfort by not asking for what you need.

 THE REALITY: YOU HAVE THE RIGHT TO ASK FOR WHAT YOU NEED.

Just like you have the right to ask for what you need, so does everyone else. However, there will be times when your needs are not aligned with each other. In these situations, it's okay to say no. If you're constantly giving in to what others need, your needs will take a backseat. It's healthy to set boundaries to maintain a balance of give-and-take in the relationship.

THE REALITY: IT'S OKAY TO SAY NO AND SET BOUNDARIES.

MYTH #4: NOTHING IS IN MY CONTROL.

You cannot control how other people behave, no matter how hard you try. In fact, people tend to avoid those who try to control other people. But, you can control your own behavior by using effective ways to respond. Passive ways can lead to you being unsatisfied, whereas aggressive ways can cause people to avoid you in the long run.

So what should you do, then? You should use assertive communication.

Assertive communication is a balance between passive and aggressive communication. It's about combining the compassion of passive strategies and the persistence of aggressive ones in a way that can address both your needs. It leads to lesser conflicts, quick resolutions and is the most effective way to communicate.

THE REALITY: YOU CAN CONTROL YOUR OWN BEHAVIOR BY CHOOSING EFFECTIVE MEANS OF COMMUNICATION.

Program 7: Malware

No matter how hard you try to communicate effectively, others may use aggressive strategies in relationships. They may play blame games, emotionally blackmail or send you on guilt trips whenever there is a conflict. The best solution is to stay away from them.

However, sometimes you can't stay away from them; they may be an integral part of your life. In these situations, there are two things that you can do:

Prepare yourself for it: Take a few deep breaths to calm down before dealing with them using Wise Mind or breathing exercises.

Watch out for their red flags: Make a note of their red flags and signs of when they're about to get aggressive. Depending on the situation, you can use any of the scripts you'll learn at the Hexagon of Hacks to deal with them.

Press Esc to exit Hurdle Heptagon.

Cave completed. Don't forget to fill in the shape.

Esc

Hexagon of Hacks

Function: To learn skills to communicate effectively.

Number of programs: 6

Welcome to the Hexagon of Hacks.

The time has come to learn effective communication skills.

But first, you need to familiarize yourself with the rights[1] that you as a person are entitled to in a relationship.

When you are in a relationship, you are entitled to the following:

1. The right to need things from other people

2. The right to prioritize yourself sometimes

3. The right to have emotions and express them

4. The right to have the final say on how you feel

5. The right to have your own opinions

6. The right to experience the world in your own unique way

7. The right to resist treatment that doesn't feel good

8. The right to a negotiation for change

9. The right to ask for something (and not always get it)

10. The right to say no

11. The right to not have to:

    (a) Justify yourself

    (b) Take responsibility for someone else's problem

    (c) Respond in a situation

Now that you're aware of what your rights are, you can proceed.

[1]Adapted from McKay et al., 1983

Program 1: Need Recognition

The first step to effective communication is to know what your needs are. If you're unsure about what you want, you'll have trouble articulating it to the other person. Here's a little exercise that you can use to recognize what you need from the other person.

Think of a relationship in which you feel like something is lacking. Observe the emotion that comes along with it.

Use the emotion directory to figure out how you're feeling and describe it:

_____

_____

_____

_____

How do you want the other person to change? (for example, stop leaving my texts on seen)	
Increase	
Decrease	
Stop	

Start	
When?	
Where?	
How often?	

Now, form a sentence summing everything up:

_____

_____

_____

_____

_____

Program 2: Pressure modulation

You know what you want, but you're not sure how forceful you should be while asking for it.

Your friend has borrowed a video game from you. You want it back. However, your friend has just experienced a loss. This may be an inappropriate time to be adamant about getting your game back.

But if they borrowed a school book that you need for an upcoming exam, it's okay to ask for it, as long as you're gentle.

On the other hand, if your friend is not in a vulnerable place and refuses to return your schoolbook, then it's okay to be forceful while asking for it.

It sounds like a lot to remember and think about. Don't worry, here's a formula you can use:

When and how to ask for something depends on your need's urgency and the other person's vulnerability. Use these two scales to judge them:

I need: _____

How urgent is my need?											
Not urgent	1	2	3	4	5	6	7	8	9	10	Very urgent

How vulnerable is the other person?											
Very vulnerable	1	2	3	4	5	6	7	8	9	10	Not vulnerable

Now add the two numbers: _____

The higher the number, the more force you can apply. If the number is low, you need to be more considerate while making your request.

Now try applying this to a recent interaction when you asked for something, but it didn't go too well.

Describe the situation:

Was the intensity too high or too low?   ☐ TOO HIGH   ☐ TOO LOW

What would you have done differently if you applied this skill?

Keep in mind that the scale for urgency is from low to high (1 is lowest), and the scale for vulnerability is from high to low (1 is highest).

Think of the 1 like the Ace in a pack of cards. With urgency, Ace represents 1, and with vulnerability, Ace is above the King.

URGENCY   VULNERABILITY

| A | 2 | 3 | 4 | 5 | 6 | 7 | 8 | 9 | 10 | J | Q | K | A |

Program 3: Simple-request formula

People need to make small and simple requests very often.

Making change for the bus

Asking for help while carrying something heavy

Finding out where the restroom is in a restaurant

Here's a formula to help you make one. Let's say you're carrying a lot of books and your shoelaces have come undone. You need someone to hold your books while you pause to tie them.

Part	Function	Example
The reason (if necessary)	This sets the scene and lets them know why you need their assistance.	My shoelaces have come undone, and I need to tie them.
The cushion	A few short words to be polite; to differentiate the request from a command.	Would you be able to...
The actual request	Be straightforward and specific about what you want: one request, when you want it, and for how long.	...hold these books for a minute so I can tie my shoelaces?
A sign of gratitude	This offers the person gratitude for taking the time out to help you.	It would really help me out. Thanks.

Full sentence: Hi, my shoelaces have come undone, and I need to tie them. Would you be able to hold these books for a minute so I can tie them? It would really help me out.

215

Here are two situations. Use the formula to come up with the request. For the last worksheet, think of a situation as well.

Situation: Asking someone to turn the volume down while you're studying

The reason (optional)	
The cushion	
Actual request	
Sign of gratitude	

Full sentence:

Situation: Enquiring when the next bus is arriving

The reason (optional)	
The cushion	
Actual request	
Sign of gratitude	

Full sentence:

Situation:

The reason (optional)	
The cushion	
Actual request	
Sign of gratitude	

Full sentence:

Remember that, according to the rights, if you make a small request, the other person has the right to say no. However, when you make a polite and well-thought-out request, the chances of a positive response are higher.

Try the script out by making small requests through the next week. Ask for directions or the time, even if you don't need to. Ask a classmate or sibling for help with something. Try the script out and see how it works out for you.

Program 4: Assertive communication

ASSERTIVE OUTPUT

Remember this?

PASSIVE	AGGRESSIVE

Being assertive is finding the balance between aggressive and passive ways of communicating. You're asking for your needs, but you're also taking into account their needs and emotions.

You can practice assertiveness by using this formula. It can also help you prepare for a difficult conversation.

A couple of examples:

1. You want to ask your parents if you can get a part time job after school.

2. The barista at the cafe has accidentally charged you for whipped cream, which you didn't ask for.

PART 1: I think _____

Description:	Start the conversation by focusing on the facts of the situation from your point of view by saying, "I think ____." This part should not include any emotions or judgments.	
Do not	Attack	"I think you've been very unfair..."
	Make assumptions	"I think you're just punishing me by..."
Example 1	I think I have some free time after school that I would like to put to use.	
Example 2	I think you've charged me for some whipped cream which I didn't ask for.	

218

Description:	This part should communicate how you feel about the situation and include an emotion.	
Do **not**	Accuse the other person	"You don't understand me." "Instead, use: I feel misunderstood."
	Make a 'You' statement that sounds like an 'I' statement	"I feel that you are cruel." "Instead, use: I feel hurt."
Example 1	I feel bored, like I'm wasting my time.	
Example 2	This is a component you use with someone close to you. The barista doesn't need to know how you feel.	

PART 3: I want _____

Description:	This part should communicate what you want to change about the situation. Use the guidelines to form this part.	
Guidelines	Ask for a change in behavior, not attitude	Asking for a change in attitude will require the other person to alter their beliefs and emotions, which may not be in their direct control. Asking for a change in behavior will be easier for them to implement.
	Ask for one thing at a time	Giving someone a list of things to change may stress and annoy them. Think of one thing that's most important to you and ask for that.
	Ask for something that can be done immediately.	Asking them to implement the change the following week or month may cause them to forget about it and upset you again.
	Be as specific as you can.	A request like 'I want you to be more caring' has room for misinterpretation. But a direct ask like 'I want you to hug me more often' is something specific that they can replicate.

| Example 1 | I want to get a part-time job after school. |
| Example 2 | I want you to correct the bill. |

PART 4: I can _____ (optional)

Description:	This part lets the other person know that you can meet them halfway; and that you're being considerate of their situation. It can also be used to convey that the change you want is significant to you. And that you'll be making alternate arrangements if they can't accommodate you.
You can use this part to:	Let them know your alternate plan if they cannot fulfill your request. (If you can't do this, I will....) Let them know that you're willing to make an effort on your end so that they may be able to fulfill your request.
Example 1	I can also contribute a little to the household expenses.
Example 2	[optional] You can take your time; I'm not in a hurry.

Full sentence

Example 1	I think I have some free time after school that I would like to put to use. I feel bored, like I'm wasting my time. I want to get a part-time job after school. I can also contribute a little to the household expenses.
Example 2	I think you've charged me for some whipped cream which I didn't ask for. I want you to correct the bill, please. You can take your time; I'm not in a hurry.

Try this exercise with three problems that you'd like to address in your life. It can be a change you want in your homelife, within your friend circle or at school.

The issue:

The changes you want:

Pick one specific change that you can ask for right away:

Form your assertive statement:

I think

I feel

I want

I can

Full sentence:

The issue:

The changes you want:

Pick one specific change that you can ask for right away:

Form your assertive statement:

I think

I feel

I want

I can

Full sentence:

The issue:

The changes you want:

Pick one specific change that you can ask for right away:

Form your assertive statement:

I think

I feel

I want

I can

Full sentence:

You've learned to complete one part of assertive communication, the output. Now you will learn the skill of assertive input or assertive listening.

It sounds a bit weird, doesn't it? To assertively listen? Isn't listening the part of communication where you don't have much to do? In reality, listening is as lively an activity as speaking is.

What did you learn to communicate in assertive output?	
I think	Your thoughts and perceptions about the situation
I feel	How you're feeling about the situation
I want	What you'd like to change about the situation
I can	How you're going to prioritize your needs and boundaries

Similarly, when another person is speaking, you need to listen to more than just the sound of their words.

You need to listen to their

- Thoughts and perceptions
- Emotions
- Wants
- Needs and boundaries

A part of assertive listening is to also ask questions when you haven't fully understood the above. Here are some examples of questions that you can use to clarify any doubts that you have:

Thoughts and perceptions	What are your thoughts on this? What do you think of _____?

Emotions	How does it make you feel when _____?
	How do you feel about this?
	Are you comfortable with this idea?
Wants	What would you like to do about this?
	What do you think we should do about this?
	How do you think we should change the situation?
Needs and boundaries	Will you be okay with _____?
	Are you sure you're okay with this?
	Is there anything troubling you?
	Can I help you with _____?

Remember that assertive listening doesn't include giving the other person what they need. It is to help you gain a better understanding of what they need, the same way that you offered clarity on your needs. This can help you arrive at a solution that takes into account both your needs.

Program 5: Listening firewalls

It sounds easy to listen attentively and gather these details. However, you may come across some firewalls that may prevent you from listening assertively.

Check the ones that you have come across.

- [ ] **Mind reading:** Making assumptions about what the other person feels or thinks without asking them.

- [ ] **Rehearsing:** Being occupied with thinking of how to respond instead of listening to the other person, who's still talking.

- [ ] **Filtering:** Taking into account or paying attention only to what's important to you.

- [ ] **Judging:** Criticizing their world view instead of trying to understand it.

- [ ] **Daydreaming:** Getting lost in your thoughts instead of paying attention to what they're saying.

- [ ] **Advising:** Offering advice instead of empathy and support.

- [ ] **Sparring:** Disqualifying the other person's views by trying to debate them.

- [ ] **Wanting to be right:** Overlooking anything they say that's critical of you or implies that you're wrong.

- [ ] **Derailing:** Changing the topic to avoid talking about something that makes you uncomfortable.

- [ ] **Appeasing:** Agreeing to what they say too quickly without actually listening to their concerns.

Now, apply this skill to recent situations when you experienced a communication breakdown.

Describe the situation	Which firewall did you encounter?	What questions could you have asked to assertively listen?

Program 6: Saying no

Saying no is an essential part of communication. If you weren't able to say no, there would be utter chaos. It would be free reign for all, and you'd spend a lot of time doing things you don't want to do.

Yet, people are afraid to say no. They fear that the other person may feel bad or that they're being selfish. But, remember clause 10 from the rights in a relationship. You have the right to say no. And you can say it assertively as well.

There are only two components to saying no effectively:

1. Offering validation to the other person's request.

2. Being clear about not wanting to do it.

Here are some everyday situations in which it may be awkward to say no:

Situation: A friend wants to meet you, but you're not in the mood.

What you can say: "I know that it's been a while since we spent time together (validation), but I'd prefer to stay in tonight (clear preference)"

Situation: Somebody offers you something to eat that you don't want to eat.

What you can say: "It's really nice of you to think of me (validation). However, I'm not hungry at the moment (clear preference)."

Situation: Remember the friend who wanted to play a racing game instead of an FPS?

What you can say: "That game is nice, and I know you really enjoy it, but I'd prefer to play an FPS this evening."

Here are a few things to keep in mind:

- Don't offer too much of a justification. Keep it as straightforward as possible.
- Do not argue. A polite refusal is to avoid an escalation of any sort.
- You're not denying them anything. You're making your need or boundary clear by stating your preference.

Sharpening your assertiveness skills

You've learned a lot of skills at the Hexagon and may be itching to try them out. But, take it slow.

Try applying these skills in low-anxiety situations at first and then move up the ladder.

Make a list of situations in which you'd like to say no, make a change or set limits. Then rank the situations from 1-10. 1 should be an easy harmless situation like telling a friend you don't want to hang out that day.

A situation ranked 10 would be an important conversation, like telling your parents you don't want to play baseball anymore.

Rank	Situation
1	
2	
3	
4	
5	
6	
7	
8	
9	
10	

Now, you can attempt to put your plan into action by tackling them one by one, going from 1 to 10.

- 💬 Make the statement you want to use
- 💬 Spend some time rehearsing it
- 💬 Think of a time and place you'd like to do it
- 💬 Make a commitment to do it

The situation	Date and time	Place

Press Esc to exit Hexagon of Hacks.

Cave completed. Don't forget to fill in the shape.

Esc

Conflict cross|

Function: To learn to deal with communication breakdown

Number of errors found: 5

You've learned the skills for both assertive input and output.

But these skills aren't taught in schools and universities, so others may not know them.

They may use aversive strategies in their communication which can cause conflict.

There are five techniques that you can use to address conflict and avoid a communication breakdown.

Mutual validation

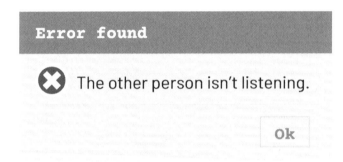

Error found

❌ The other person isn't listening.

Ok

One of the reasons this happens is because the other person feels undermined. They may feel that you don't understand where they're coming from, how they feel, and what they need. So they may unnecessarily bombard you with arguments and accusations.

In this situation, you can use mutual validation to acknowledge their experience. Remember clause 6 of the rights in a relationship. You have the right to experience the world in your own unique way. And so do they.

To use mutual validation, you need to:

1. Empathize with their feelings

2. State your own predicament

A few examples

> I understand that we're a family of athletes. On my end, I feel that my skills are more in tune with the debate team, and I'd enjoy it more than baseball.

> I understand that you feel hurt by my need to decline your invitation. On my end, it's been a busy week with assignments, and I'd prefer to rest this weekend. Perhaps, we can do something another time?

Output repetition

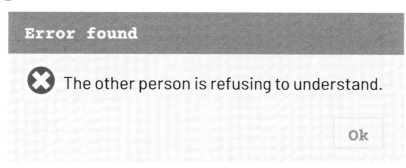

Error found

❌ The other person is refusing to understand.

Ok

They may keep asking questions to derail the conversation or blatantly ignore your request. This can cause frustration and anger.

The way to resist this is to keep calm and continue to make your request by just changing a word here and there or rephrasing it.

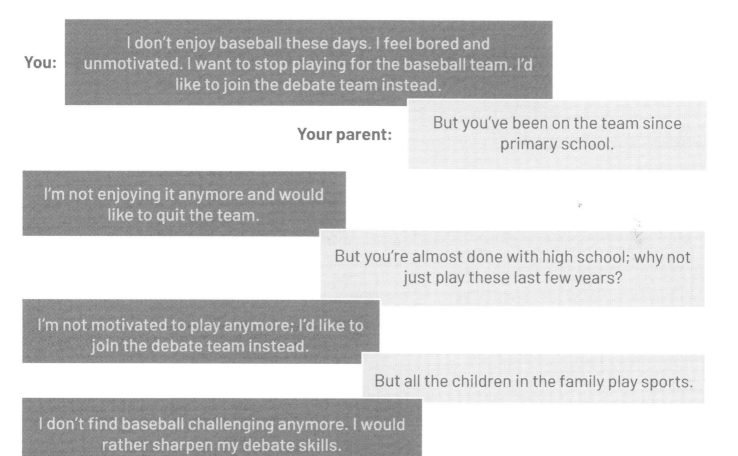

You: I don't enjoy baseball these days. I feel bored and unmotivated. I want to stop playing for the baseball team. I'd like to join the debate team instead.

Your parent: But you've been on the team since primary school.

I'm not enjoying it anymore and would like to quit the team.

But you're almost done with high school; why not just play these last few years?

I'm not motivated to play anymore; I'd like to join the debate team instead.

But all the children in the family play sports.

I don't find baseball challenging anymore. I would rather sharpen my debate skills.

You may feel the urge to respond to their questions or dispute their statements. This can escalate the situation and turn the focus away from what you want to communicate.

Input verification

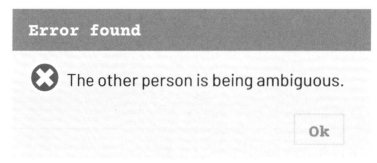

Another obstacle that you can run into is when someone is being vague about their request.

For example

Someone tells you that you're not being a good friend.

It's a vague statement and doesn't specifically point out what they need from you. Here are some questions you could ask them in this situation:

- What is it that makes me a bad friend?
- What would you like me to do to be a better friend?
- Can you give me an example of why I'm not being a good friend?
- How should I have reacted when I (example)?

This method is to ask questions until you get to the underlying emotion, perception, or need that the other person is trying to communicate.

Assertive sleep mode

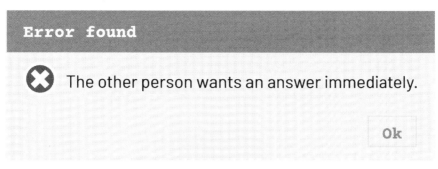

Error found

❌ The other person wants an answer immediately.

Ok

Sometimes they may want you to come to a conclusion right away. They might insist on you making a decision or agreeing with them immediately.

In this situation, simply assert yourself and take a time-out.

> You've shared a lot with me. I need some time to think about it and make a decision.

During the time-out, you can think about both your needs. You can use a script to form a calm and assertive response and then come back to the discussion. By that time, the other person would have also had time to calm down.

Assertive compliance

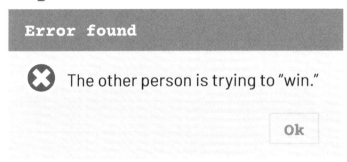

Error found

❌ The other person is trying to "win."

Ok

The purpose of negotiation is to find a solution that caters to both parties. However, some people will try to 'win' the argument.

For example

One night, you come home late. Your parent says:

You always come late.

In this situation, you are indeed late. But the 'always' is an exaggeration and can escalate the situation into an argument.

So, you can agree in part to what they're saying; and ignore the aggressive bit.

Yes, I agree that I'm late on occasion.

This removes the possibility of a 'win' because you're agreeing with them. The heat escapes from the situation, and a negotiation can take place.

Press Esc to exit Conflict Cross.

Cave completed. Don't forget to fill in the shape.

Esc

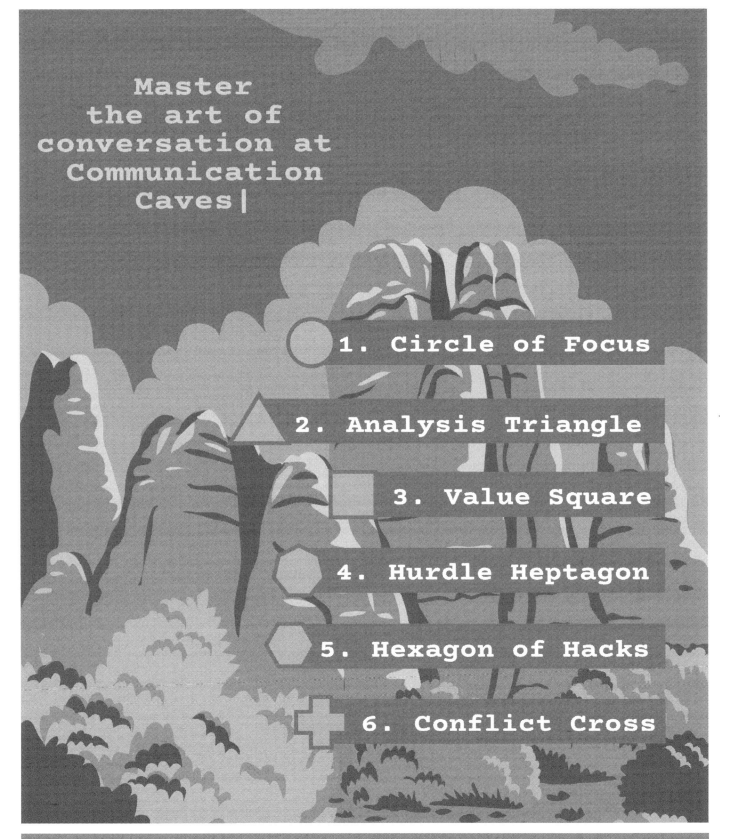

Master
the art of
conversation at
Communication
Caves|

1. Circle of Focus

2. Analysis Triangle

3. Value Square

4. Hurdle Heptagon

5. Hexagon of Hacks

6. Conflict Cross

Congratulations!

Well done, human. You've completed all the programs at Communication Caves.

Continue to reward

This is to certify that

_____

has completed the quest:

'Master the art of conversation'

at Communication Caves

on_____

Beep.

Signed

Captcha

You've learned the essentials of human communication.

Listening
Communication blocks
Effective communication
Conflict management

I'll now disclose the hidden files - The Raven ▪

While trying to settle a conflict, the starting position is that both parties' needs are valid.

The Raven is a hidden file that holds the secret to negotiation. A negotiation is a discussion that is had when two parties are in disagreement to come up with a compromise.
But before you begin the negotiation, remember the following:

- Stay relaxed. Do some of the exercises that you learned at Emotion Island. They will help the heat of the emotion escape so you can enter the negotiation calm and composed.

- Remember the obsolete modes at Obstacle Obtagon? Give them a read before you start negotiating so you can avoid using them.

- Their needs are as real as yours. If you are unclear on their needs, clarify them and then, validate them. You need to take both your needs into account while coming up with a compromise.

- At Value Square, you had to reflect on the values that you would like to have, in a relationship. Examine these values and see if you can come up with a compromise that meets them.

- Raised voices, anger and tones of judgement have no place in a negotiation. They will likely keep you in a state of conflict. Speak in a low volume, using a neutral voice.

It's a bit of a long list, so you can remember it by thinking of The Raven.

R Relax

a Avoid aversive strategies

v Validate their needs

e Examine your values

n Neutral voice

With the Raven in mind, you can begin the process of negotiation.

In a negotiation, you need to take turns and offer solutions. Remember that the solution you offer MUST address some of their needs. If you don't know what those needs are, clarify by asking questions.

When many solutions come up—some yours, some theirs—it's time to find a compromise.

Compromise techniques|

I'll cut the cake; you get the first piece

You and your sibling have collected PC games over the years; however, they're leaving for university and want to take the games with them.

You can suggest that one of you divides the games into two piles, and the other gets the first chance to choose which pile they can take.

If the person who gets to divide the games puts all the good ones in one pile, the other will simply choose that pile and take it. So, they have to make sure that both the piles are equal in quality.

This way, both you and your sibling get an equal share of the collection.

Taking turns

You and your sibling share a bunk bed. You both like to sleep on the upper bunk. You decide to take turns to sleep on the upper bunk.

Do both

You want to go bowling; your friend wants to go to the beach. You decide to do both!

Trial period

You and your sibling have a problem but two different solutions to it. You agree to use their solution for a stipulated period of time, after which you'll open up the discussion again. If either of you is unhappy with the solution, you renegotiate.

To each their own

When you're cleaning the room, you prefer to tidy up the place by collecting everything on your table and then putting them back to where they belong.

Your sibling, however, prefers to tidy up by putting everything back to where they belong, one by one.

You compromise by agreeing to clean the room your way when it's your turn, and they can clean it their way when it's their turn

Tit for tat

You think your sibling should keep the room cleaner. They think that you should wipe down the bathroom floor after you use it.

You say that you'll wipe down the bathroom floor if they agree to keep the room cleaner.

Part of what I want with part of what you want

You like Italian food, but your sibling likes Chinese, and this always causes conflict while getting takeout.

Get both; a little bit of Chinese and a little bit of Italian.

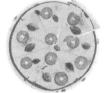

Split the difference

You and your sibling go to the beach. They want to spend four hours there. You'd like to leave earlier, after only two hours.

You split the difference and decide to spend three hours instead. That way, they get to spend some extra time, but you also get to leave early.

Think of a recent conflict you had with someone because you had different needs. Describe the situation. Then, come up with two compromises that you could have suggested using the techniques above.

Situation	Compromise you could have made
1.	
2.	
3.	

Analyzing problem interactions|

Now you've learned everything you can about communication. However, it'll still be hard for you to implement these immediately and see quick results. You may continue to use obsolete modes of conflict resolution.

You may explode with anger at the end of a fight or find shelter by isolating yourself in your room. But you can learn from them and sharpen your communication skills.

Here's a Communication Effectiveness Checklist that you can use to analyze interactions and improve them.

Communication Effectiveness Checklist

Describe the situation:

Were you clear about the following?

Your goals	☐ YES	☐ NO
What you wanted	☐ YES	☐ NO
What you didn't want	☐ YES	☐ NO
Your values	☐ YES	☐ NO

Did you use any of these aversive strategies?

Discounting	☐
Leaving	☐
Threatening	☐
Belittling	☐
Blaming	☐
Guilt-tripping	☐
Derailing	☐
Appeasing	☐

Did you use any passive strategies?

Avoiding ☐

Isolating ☐

What were the obstacles you faced?

Emotion overload ☐

Need recognition failure ☐

What-ifs ☐

Myth #1: It is wrong to want anything in a relationship. ☐

Myth #: Rejection, disappointment, and anger are unbearable. ☐

Myth #3: Saying no is not an option. ☐

Myth #4: Nothing is in my control. ☐

Malware ☐

Was there faulty intensity modulation?

☐ TOO HIGH   ☐ TOO LOW

Did you run into any hurdles while being assertive?

Using judgments instead of facts ☐

Making a 'you' statement instead of an 'I' statement ☐

Not being specific about the change you want ☐

Did you experience any listening firewalls?

Mind reading ☐

Rehearsing ☐

Filtering ☐

Judging ☐

Daydreaming ☐

Advising ☐

Sparring ☐

Wanting to be right ☐

Derailing ☐

Appeasing ☐

Did you use a conflict management strategy?

Mutual validation ☐

Output repetition ☐

Input verification ☐

Assertive sleep mode ☐

Assertive compliance ☐

Did you use the Raven?

☐ YES   ☐ NO

Did you use a compromise strategy?

☐ YES   ☐ NO

Press Esc to Exit

Esc

Well, human, it's time for you to leave. I would miss you, but I don't have the sufficient parts to do so. I do wish you the best. Goodbye.

This is to certify that

_____

has completed all the quests

and has learned the following skills:

Inner focus

Distress endurance

Emotional regulation

Effective communication

on _____

CONGRATULATIONS

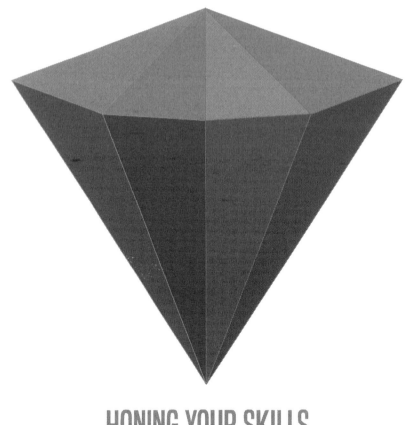

HONING YOUR SKILLS

You've completed all the quests and collected your rewards. You've gained invaluable lessons in focus, coping, emotional regulation, and communication, which will serve you well for life.

But like any other skill, you need to practice them so they remain sharp. With enough practice, they will eventually become second nature to you.

You did many exercises during your journey. Some of them were to bring your attention to how your mind works.

Some exercises were for self-observation and techniques that you could use in your daily life. Here is a chart of the exercises you can use, what you can use them for, and the page number where you can find them.

MINDFULNESS MOUNTAIN

Distress Desert

Emotion Island

Communication Caves

REFERENCES

Dialectical Behavior Therapy. (2020, June 1).
    DBT : Dialectical Behavior Therapy - Skills, Worksheets, & Videos. DBT.
    https://dialecticalbehaviortherapy.com/

Linehan, M. M. (2015).
    DBT® Skills Training Handouts and Worksheets, Second Edition (Second
    Edition, (Spiral-Bound Paperback) ed.). The Guilford Press.

McKay, M., Wood, J. C., & Brantley, J. (2007).
    *The Dialectical Behavior Therapy Skills Workbook: Practical DBT Exercises
    for Learning Mindfulness, Interpersonal Effectiveness, Emotion Regulation
    & ... (A New Harbinger Self-Help Workbook)* (1st ed.). New
    Harbinger Publications.

VanMuijen, A., Valerie, E., Margo, S., & Michelle, M. G. (2020).
    The 2020 emotion wheel [Illustration]. https://www.avanmuijen.com/
    watercolor-emotion-wheel

A SHORT MESSAGE FROM TEEN THRIVE

Hi there. We hope you enjoyed the book.

We would love to hear your thoughts on the book.

Many readers don't know how hard reviews are to come by,
and how much they help an author.

We would be incredibly grateful if you could take just 60 seconds to write a
short review on Amazon, even if it's just a sentence or two!

Log on to www.teen-thrive.com/review for instructions
on how to leave a review.

Thank you for taking the time to share your thoughts.
Every single review makes a difference to us.

Printed in Great Britain
by Amazon

69168654R00149